Crystal Rituals

BY THE MOON

Crystal Rituals

BY THE MOON

RAISING YOUR VIBRATION
THROUGH EVERY LUNAR CYCLE

LEAH SHOMAN

ROCKPOOL

A Rockpool book
PO Box 252
Summer Hill
NSW 2130
Australia

rockpoolpublishing.com
Follow us! f ⓘ rockpoolpublishing
Tag your images with #rockpoolpublishing

ISBN: 9781925946840

Published in 2022 by Rockpool Publishing

Design by Sara Lindberg, Rockpool Publishing
Edited by Heather Millar

 A catalogue record for this
book is available from the
National Library of Australia

Printed and bound in China
10 9 8 7 6 5 4 3 2 1

Contents

Introduction

Healing with crystals

My name is Leah and I have unintentionally been using crystals my entire existence, and intentionally, for the past decade. What I mean when I say I was unintentionally using crystals is that, ever since I can remember, I have always been drawn to crystals, rocks and mineral specimens. I would hold them, stare at them, bask in their beauty and all they had to offer – and yet I knew nothing of what they were actually giving me at that time. All I knew was, they invoked a certain feeling within me, they called to me, but I couldn't quite hear them yet.

It took a lot of struggling; it took a lot of pain; it took many failed karmic relationships; and it took enduring emotional, mental, physical and sexual abuse to lead me to where I am today. What we often don't recognise is that going through these abusive episodes stores trauma and a specific low vibrational energy within our bodies. To release this trauma, we must go within to begin to heal these wounds and raise our vibration to align with our higher selves. Leaning into the healing power of crystals led me to this specific soul mission, in this lifetime, to reawaken to my crystal guardian powers and to spread the knowledge I have obtained to the collective.

After three decades of knowing that there was something *more* intended for my life, that there was something *bigger* I was meant to be doing, it finally *clicked*. Like my spirit guides always said, it will be that lightbulb moment, and it was. I *knew* I had to work with crystals in any and all capacities – enter Dark Moon Crystals.

I started Dark Moon Crystals – my energy healing practice and crystal boutique – on a whim, following my intuition. I remember the day as if it were yesterday, as it was such a pivotal shift in my journey. I remember how my body was beyond tired of the everyday life I had fallen into. I was tired of working hard to run someone else's company when I could be putting all my time, effort and energy into my own and into something I truly loved – something that set my soul on fire. So, I asked myself, 'Why *can't* I do this?' I continued to psych myself up, because I was terrified of failing, and then I purchased my ABN. From that moment on, crystals and I became bound, yet again, together in this lifetime and the rest to come.

Crystals are in my every day and every minute of my life. If I'm not physically holding one, packing them for my beautiful customers or using them in healings and meditations, they are stationed in every single location imaginable in my home, purse and on my being. Crystals and I have a special bond, a bond that brings me so much joy and allows me to harness my intuition. Their presence is one that I would not enjoy living without. I reincarnated back into this lifetime with a specific mission at hand, and that is to match individuals with their energetically aligned crystals and infuse them further with the power and frequencies I have been gifted with and to *heal* the collective with these crystals and gifts.

What you will gather about me after reading this book is that I'm all about research and expanding my wealth of knowledge about, well… everything, but especially crystals. I get this information downloaded from Source and my spirit guides, but also through my own knowledge that has been embedded within my DNA. When I come in contact with a crystal, it's as if I am constantly re-awakening to its properties and energy.

I created this book to spread the knowledge I have obtained through my own healing journey, as well as to inspire and motivate the collective into connecting to themselves and Source on a deeper, more authentic level. I want to show that we can all harness the potential and power that Mother Earth has so generously offered us, and in so doing, we can *heal, evolve and grow* into our highest selves. When we equip ourselves with the power of knowledge, there are pathways that become illuminated and universal doorways that begin to open to us.

This is a book to inform, to unlock the sacred knowledge and to enhance your relationship with the natural properties all around us. When we begin using crystals with intent, the magic begins to unfold; the veil between this realm and the next becomes thinner, and we can tap into our ever-growing potential. One thing I know for certain is I am as much their guardian as they are mine.

Crystals are ancient and are one of the most widely utilised methods of achieving this state of transcendence, where the mind is free to roam to places beyond our human awareness. Crystals are infused with millions of years of sacred knowledge and hold the high-frequency energies of Earth upon their formation.

You can think of crystals almost like a self-learning super brain, as they hold, remember, store and absorb information on touch, which I like to call energy transference. When you handle, hold or touch a crystal, it is imparting this knowledge to you.

Ancient civilisations used crystals for protection, healings and other institutions of divination. These ancients innately knew the power of crystals that we are now re-awakening to. They were aware of the beneficial energy brought forth by placing crystals in their sacred spaces and altars, or simply wearing them. When these energies come in contact with our own vibrational frequencies, shifts begin to occur. We can raise our vibrational output simply by being near these crystals.

Each crystal is uniquely its own and operates on different frequencies, some have a stronger output whereas others may have a softer and gentler hum. Nonetheless, they all have their purpose. If you are a beginner with crystals or have been using them your entire life, you will learn to navigate their frequencies and metaphysical properties once you attune with what your etheric and physical body are calling for.

Crystals are beautiful gifts that Mother Earth has imparted to us, and they are in fact a gift that keeps on giving, for crystals emit certain healing vibrations and frequencies that are quite beneficial to our human systems. Many of you out there may already be in tune with a crystal's energy, which is fantastic, but for others the process can be quite arduous and overwhelming, and at times, you can become defeated when you don't feel what others feel or experience their energy in the same way. I know this from personal experience, as I know and can recognise that I contain great power within my own human system, but yet I am so accustomed to the energies already soaring through me that I cannot always identify them.

Don't be fooled by thoughts that you're not *feeling* these energies – this is just your ego and conscious mind stepping in and telling you it can't see it so it's not there. If you feel as if you have never and will never feel their energy, I'm going to tell you, you are wrong. I am here to reaffirm to you that you already contain the power within you to feel a crystal's energy; it's just a matter of beginning to reawaken to these abilities. The more you work with your crystals, the deeper your connection will become, and it will be easier to sense and feel their energy.

Some helpful tips for your healing journey with crystals:

- Release the pressure and expectations you are placing on yourself.
- Remember that there is literally no right or wrong way to reawaken to your abilities.
- Energy from crystals can be subtle and at times hard to recognise, so again, refer to the first point in this list and release the pressure from yourself – as you begin to reawaken you will be able to pick up on these energies.
- Practise, practise and practise some more. The more you practise feeling into your crystals' energy and trust your intuition, the quicker you will be able to recognise and feel without even realising that you are.

My healing journey with crystals

I started my own personal healing journey by doing some deep shadow work, to address the abuse and trauma I had experienced in the past, and that I was still living through on a daily basis being triggered by normal day-to-day life interactions and activities. These experiences had been embedded deeply within me, and I had to find a way to rid myself of the negative energies and entities that had been stored in my body through experiencing this trauma, so I began to practise breathwork, meditation with crystals, as well as crystal healings, by gridding with crystals on my physical body and etheric body.

When we go through a traumatic experience or there has been a damaging blow to our psyche, these experiences are held within the human system. For instance, I had been pushed onto a metal bed frame during a fight with an ex-partner. This not only caused what I thought would be permanent physical damage to my back, but it also wounded me emotionally and mentally. Someone who said they loved me and wanted to take care of me was then verbally,

mentally and physically harming me. The next day I was a complete mess. My eyes were swollen from crying from pain and fear for my life. My back was so badly damaged I could barely drive my car or walk through the door at work. Months later, I still didn't have full mobility, and I would experience pain all day and night. I was extremely uncomfortable in every sense possible and felt utterly defeated. More fights ensued. I was subjected to more verbal, mental and physical abuse. Being told no one would ever want me again. Being called a slut because I bent down to tie my shoe in public, which clearly meant I wanted people to watch me bend over. Being controlled in every single aspect – who I spoke to, what I wore and where I could go. All of these experiences stayed with me. I became extremely thin. I couldn't remember the last time I smiled and didn't cry. I was mentally, emotionally and physically exhausted.

Finally, I left for good. I wouldn't allow myself to remain in this karmic cycle of hell. I knew I had learned from this experience. I knew that I would end up dead if I stayed. I knew I wouldn't and couldn't be *myself* anymore. So, I began the healing process with the help of a dear friend. Since this was not my first experience with abuse, these negative energies were deeply engrained within me and not only affected me emotionally and mentally, but they also manifested physically with a wounded womb and endometriosis, with my back pain, with my weight, and with a lot of my chakras being blocked, unbalanced and not activated. It was as if I had to relearn who I was all over again, and my crystals helped me do this.

I began using crystals as a healing tool, to get back to my old self or better yet, an upgraded version, by placing crystals on and around my body (gridding). This crystal healing process allowed me to release the negative energies within my systems so I could *heal* from the inside out. Once I began to address the trauma and release these negative energies, the way in which my injuries and pain had physically manifested began to dissipate. I was actively activating my etheric body and human system to work in unison and to begin to heal and regenerate itself, as it had been stagnating for a long time. When I was able to allow new energy and light to run through, I was experiencing life again for the first time and connecting with my higher self, my soul and its purpose, and I began the ever-growing connection with Source and my spirit guides.

Now, I would like to share this process with you. I perform these healings still on myself as often as possible, especially when feeling blocked, and also with clients of Dark Moon Crystals. This is a process of trusting yourself, trusting what your intuition and body is telling you, without using any words, rather by tapping into all of your senses and emotions.

Harnessing the power of the lunar cycles with crystals

Do you ever feel like you don't ever get what you want? What if that's just an illusion you're allowing yourself to see, and you *actually do* receive what you ask for – it's just in an unexpected form? Once I stopped believing that nothing goes my way, I began to reflect on *what has*, and I began to shift my perspective. I began to think about the times I thought that I couldn't manifest, but in reality, that's exactly what I was doing. The universe brought me all that I asked for – I just didn't realise that it came to me in a different form.

The universe is a provider of all things, and we can ask her for anything we desire, and she will bring it to us, in one form or another. There are ways you can increase your connection with the universe, and it begins by aligning yourself energetically with the things you wish to receive. When she is ready to pass along these desires and gifts, you will be energetically on the same frequency and be open to doing so.

As my perspective shifted and as my spirituality grew – as *I* grew – and as I learned who I truly was as a human being inside and out, the bond between me and the crystals grew. We have become an unstoppable force. I started nourishing my crystals as they nourished me. I bathed them in sunlight and moonlight, gave them a purpose, as they gave to me, and started setting my intentions with them to enforce my manifestations. Since I've been utilising Mother Earth's elements and the universal forces around me, my life has become a vision of everything I wanted to receive, everything I wanted and want to be, thus far.

When new moons approach every lunar cycle, I like to reset my intentions with each of my crystals. I write down what I want to manifest and what my goals are for that month, and I hold them to my heart and speak these intentions to the crystals and keep their individual love notes

with them. I do this as a daily process to really solidify what I want the outcome to be, once these thoughts come to fruition during the full moon.

As I've let my mind expand and become open to other ways of receiving the gifts I've asked for, and the bond between myself and my crystals has evolved, I've simultaneously taken the pressure off myself and the universe to deliver my desires, instead of making it all on *my* terms (which can essentially bring upon blockages instead of manifestations).

Since I had received these gifts in an unexpected way, but I simply hadn't made the connection that this is exactly what I had asked for, I would tend to be hard on myself and ask:

'Am I not manifesting correctly?'
'Is there a *correct way* to manifest?
'Do I want it *too badly*?'

My suggestion is, *let go* of all these notions and questions. Look around you, open your eyes, ears, heart and mind just a little more and truly be open (don't just think that you are) to what you are receiving when you align yourself with the universal flow and magnetic force of your crystals. Know that you will match your energetic frequencies and attract the same vibrations in return. Be clear and firm with your intent.

PART 1:

WORKING WITH CRYSTALS

The chakra and meridian systems

There are many ways of working with crystals, but two of the main techniques I use for both my own healing and balancing and in my sessions with clients are the chakra system and the meridian system. Crystals can be used to cleanse the energetic body by placing them on the chakras and by tapping on the meridian points.

The chakra system and dimensional planes

There are 114 chakras in the human system, and although some healers like to work with twenty-two chakras, I am going to focus on the first thirteen, as going above the thirteenth is difficult for those who haven't yet opened and activated above this chakra. Chakras one to seven are your third-dimensional chakras (3D), chakras eight to fifteen are fourth-dimensional chakras (4D) and chakras sixteen to twenty-two are fifth-dimensional chakras (5D). Let's break down these dimensions:

3D – EARTHLY – MATERIAL REALM

Human level and our material world. Most humans operate on the 3D plane as a majority of the collective feel deep fear, anxiety, stress etc. Basically, falling into the drama of everyday life and letting it consume you and not allowing you to place full trust within yourself and the universe. Living in fear and the mentality of scarcity.

4D – ASTRAL PLANE – GATEWAY

When we begin to awaken to what is happening around us and the understanding that we are all interconnected, we begin to shift into the 4D level of consciousness. This is where you have the urge to follow your greatest desires and passions and where your intuition begins to grow stronger and stronger.

5D – PLANE OF LIGHT – UNCONDITIONAL LOVE

On this plane, we feel a sense of universal oneness where you feel and breed unconditional love. In this dimensional state, you can manifest quicker, and you're fully allowing the universe to work in accordance with your higher self and soul. You begin to find empowerment within yourself and within the collective. You honour your deepest truth and become connected with your truest authentic self.

Why is understanding the different dimensions important when working with crystals and the chakra system? Well, it's not only so you can have a deeper understanding of how our physical body and etheric body are intertwined and how one can adversely affect another, but when you are targeting these energetic centres with crystals, a harmonic connection occurs. We can begin to heal not only from the inside out, but we can gather the universal cosmic energy that is waiting to be tapped into.

When I practise crystal healing on my clients, I begin working with the twelve-chakra system. The twelve chakras are representative of the major energy systems located inside and outside the body. Many people work with a seven-chakra system, however, there are five other upper centres that are just as importation as the seven below them. Each of the seven chakras correspond to specific organs and nerves that pertain to the emotional body, physical body and spiritual body, and they are coded by colour. The additional five chakras, to complete the system, are located outside the human body. Energy should flow constantly through the chakras, beginning at the root chakra and travelling up through to the crown chakra, so it is essential that the chakras remain open and activated. From the crown chakra, the remaining five chakras start above the crown chakra. When a chakra is blocked, the energy flow can be restricted, which can manifest as physical, emotional or spiritual symptoms.

The twelve-chakra system is representative of universal connectedness – from being rooted through the earth chakra that travels to the core of Mother Earth below you, all the way up to the cosmos through the universal chakra above you. When you use all twelve chakras, you are then able to call in additional, powerful universal healing energies to enhance your human system.

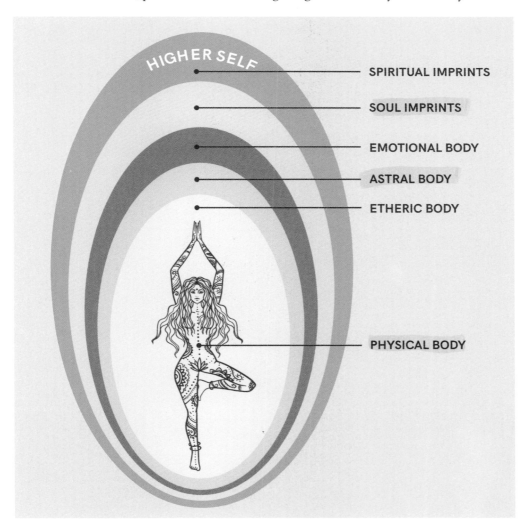

HIGHER SELF

SPIRITUAL IMPRINTS

SOUL IMPRINTS

EMOTIONAL BODY

ASTRAL BODY

ETHERIC BODY

PHYSICAL BODY

☽ 0. EARTH STAR CHAKRA ☾

Placement: 12-18 inches below the soles of your feet
Colour: brown/black
Meaning: connects and aligns your body and soul to the core of Mother Earth
Crystals to use: smoky quartz, black tourmaline

The Earth star chakra is linked to your past lives and karma, and acts as an anchor for your etheric body. It provides you with stability and grounding while deepening your ability to understand the interconnectedness of the collective and Mother Earth; and it allows you to learn from past transgressions and grow from it.

Smoky quartz – Smoky quartz is the most efficient grounding stone with strong connections to Mother Earth. She is the answer when it comes to stress, by relieving fears, helping to ease depression and standing by the mantra, 'let go of what no longer serves you'. Place smoky quartz in your home for protection and to emit positive vibrations.

Black tourmaline – Black tourmaline is a powerfully protective and grounding stone, as it shields you from negativity. It will take this negative energy and transmute it into positive energies and vibrations from your environment and person. Black tourmaline is also useful to shield psychic attacks and enforces a force field around your aura to prevent energy leakage and to repel lower energetic vibrations.

Placement: base of the tailbone/spine
Colour: red
Element: earth
Meaning: represents our root connection to the earth,
our physical bodies and our ancestors
Body part/system: male reproductive organs, adrenals, kidneys, lower spine
Crystals to use: red jasper, carnelian
Essential oils: cedarwood, black pepper, lavender, patchouli
Message: use healing mantras that begin with '*I am...*'

When the root chakra is balanced you feel safe and at home. When it is unbalanced or blocked you can feel fear and panic.

Red jasper - Red jasper strengthens and deepens your connection to Mother Earth and through this connection she allows and aids you in removing stress from your body and calming your overactive mind. Red jasper heals when working on your root and sacral chakras, helping to increase vitality, endurance and stamina, and giving you that energy boost that's been weighed down by stress and anxiety.

Carnelian - Carnelian is a stone that represents the cycle of life, death, afterlife, rebirth. Carnelian can ease your fears of the cycle of life and was used in ancient times to protect the dead. Carnelian helps with motivation and promotes making positive life choices to help you reach your goals while also restoring vitality, instilling courage and stimulating your creativity. Using carnelian during meditation helps you sink deeper and allows you to truly focus without outside interference and internal interrupting thoughts.

) 2. SWADHISTHANA: SACRAL CHAKRA (

Placement: lower abdomen below the navel and up towards the pelvic region
Colour: orange
Element: water
Meaning: represents your emotional body, creativity and sensuality
Body part/system: bladder, female reproductive organs, kidneys, large intestine
Crystals to use: tiger's eye, sunstone
Essential oils: ylang ylang, mandarin, jasmine, cardamom
Message: use healing mantras that begin with '*I feel...*'

When the sacral chakra is balanced you feel harmonious and creative, with a zest for life. When it is unbalanced or blocked you may feel unmotivated about life, sex and exercise.

Tiger's eye – Tiger's eye is a powerful stone, with a combination of earth and sun energy elements. It can help to release fears and anxiety, and in finding harmony and balance. Tiger's eye provides much-needed mental clarity for making logical decisions and clearing emotions. Place tiger's eye on the sacral chakra to ground and focus your mind.

Sunstone - Sunstone lets the real you shine, encouraging independence and originality and deepening your sense of empowerment. Sunstone allows you to look within and gives you the encouragement to say 'no' when you're feeling overwhelmed, anxious and need time to focus your energy inward. Sunstone will boost your enthusiasm and motivation and allow you to look on the brighter side of any perspective that allows your human system to stimulate self-healing.

CHAPTER 1

Placement: upper abdomen 5 cm above the navel

Colour: yellow

Element: fire

Meaning: represents the core of your identity: who you are and where you store your personal power and confidence

Body part/system: liver, gallbladder, pancreas, small intestine, stomach, upper spinal column

Crystals to use: golden healer quartz, yellow jade

Essential oils: frankincense, lemon, bergamot, juniper

Message: use healing mantras that begin with *'I do...'*

When the solar plexus chakra is balanced, you display your authentic self. When it is unbalanced or blocked, you can feel a lack of self-control and purpose in life.

Golden healer quartz – This is an extremely powerful healing crystal that sends and radiates golden healing light energy from your crown and universal chakras through to your solar plexus and spreads this healing light throughout the rest of your entire chakra system, allowing it to be unblocked and activated.

Yellow jade – Yellow jade harnesses fire energies and pushes you to be more optimistic, to gain wisdom and intellect and to further your enthusiasm for life and your work. Yellow jade brings an air of self-confidence, dispels your doubts and wards off any harmful or negative energies. Yellow jade also is said to attract good fortune, good luck and happiness; and it also heavily promotes a healthy relationship and provides you with emotional stability.

CHAPTER 1

> **Placement:** centre of the chest
> **Colour:** green
> **Element:** air
> **Meaning:** represents your emotional life, unconditional love and your astral body
> **Body part/system:** thymus gland, lungs, heart
> **Crystals to use:** moss agate, rhodonite
> **Essential oils:** may chang, rose absolute, neroli
> **Message:** use healing mantras that begin with '*I love...*'

When the heart chakra is balanced, you experience deeper love, connection and compassion. When it is unbalanced or blocked, you can act distant and unsympathetic.

Moss agate – Moss agate is the 'stone of emotional healing' and is used to resolve blockages to rebalance your heart chakra with its green crystal energy. Moss agate is here to guide you on your soul journey and aid you in finding what you need and how to understand your emotions clearly. Once you harness the energy of moss agate, you will receive its energy of success, prosperity and wealth.

Rhodonite – Rhodonite is known as the 'stone of compassion and forgiveness'. Rhodonite releases you from your emotional wounds from the past and brings emotional balance by dispelling old destructive and abusive behaviours. Rhodonite activates your heart chakra allowing you to nurture new love and not be afraid to let it in. Rhodonite provides you with her grounding energy and ensures your yin/yang are balanced, so you can hit your fullest potential.

CHAPTER 1

Placement: centre of the neck

Colour: blue

Element: ether

Body part/system: throat, thyroid, jaw, neck, mouth, lungs

Meaning: represents expressing what your authentic self needs to express and clear communication

Crystals to use: angelite, blue apatite

Essential oils: basil, sweet orange, chamomile

Message: use healing mantras that begin with '*I speak...*'

When the throat chakra is balanced, it aligns your vision with reality. When it is unbalanced or blocked, you feel small and timid.

Angelite – This is a high vibrational stone that enhances your communication and connection with your spirit guides and angels on this realm and others. Angelite will open, activate and align your throat, third-eye and crown chakras, allowing you to attune the frequency of your higher self and your divine light council. When using angelite during meditation, you can increase your verbal manifestation, as angelite helps you speak your truth and desires to the universe and assists you in making them a reality on this physical plane. The more you work with angelite, the more you will see it attuning to your vibrations and allowing you to deepen the connection with every usage.

Blue apatite – Blue apatite encourages you to grow spiritually and in your psychic gifts while encouraging your creativity and helps increase your inner strength. Blue apatite helps clear any blockages within your throat chakra and begins to rebalance it, allowing you to speak your truth and aligning you with your higher self and greatest potential.

CHAPTER 1

) 6. AJNA: THIRD-EYE CHAKRA (

Placement: slightly above the brow centre; it is connected to the pineal gland

Colour: indigo

Element: light

Body part/system: pituitary gland, eyes, brain, hormones

Meaning: represents your focus and inner vision to be able to see the bigger picture in life

Crystals to use: auralite 23, super seven

Essential oils: clary sage, rosemary, bergamot

Message: use healing mantras that begin with '*I see...*'

When the third-eye chakra is balanced, you have clear intuition and insight. When it is unbalanced or blocked, you rely more on others for clear direction.

Auralite 23 – With twenty-three magnificent minerals packed into its form, auralite 23 is revered as a powerful seeker transformer crystal. Auralite 23 works with activating and enhancing your third-eye and crown chakras and can enhance your psychic awareness. Using auralite 23 while meditating can aid in connecting you to the higher realms to meet with your higher self and your spirit guides. Auralite 23 is here for you on your journey of awakening and can provide you with the revitalisation you've been searching for physically as well as clearing out emotional baggage and triggers.

Super seven – A combination of seven crystals – amethyst, clear quartz, smoky quartz, rutilated quartz, geothite, cacoxenite and lepidocrocite – super seven contains all metaphysical properties of each crystal, which makes it a powerhouse. This crystal is here for humanity and to heal Mother Earth, and it helps you tap into your intuitive and psychic abilities. Super seven purifies and balances your chakras and your auric field, so you're able to energetically align with your higher self. Placing super seven near any other crystals will increase their vibrations.

CHAPTER 1

Placement: the top of the head
Colour: violet
Element: cosmos
Body part/system: pineal gland, spinal cord, biological cycles, brain stem
Meaning: represents self-transcendence, loss of ego, enlightened wisdom; connects your physical body to the universe and soul
Crystals to use: lepidolite, que sera
Essential oils: palo santo, lavender, lime
Message: use healing mantras that begin with '*I know...*'

When the crown chakra is balanced, you will experience enlightenment. When it is unbalanced or blocked, you fear leaving the world behind and allow ego to get in the way.

Lepidolite – Known to be the stone of transition, lepidolite brings deep emotional healing, and reduces stress, anxiety and depression, along with dissipating any negative energy so you can be the best you, you can be. Lepidolite helps you transition softly from your old behavioural patterns into ones that will serve you better. Hold lepidolite and feel her calming energy.

Que sera – Que sera, aka llanite, assists you in opening your communication with the higher realm and enhances your clairaudient abilities. Que sera has a high, powerful vibration and channels spiritual light and energy through your body and your auric field. Que sera uses this energy to balance your meridians and recharge your energy field. Although que sera resonates with all chakras, que sera resonates most deeply with the crown and soul-star chakras. Keep que sera with you to assist you in gaining awareness on your life path.

Placement: above the crown chakra - around 6 inches above your head
Colour: white
Meaning: this is where your soul resides; similar to the crown chakra but represents divine spiritual energy, connectedness to your higher self, the Akashic records and the universe; trust your path
Crystals to use: clear quartz, selenite
Message: practise gratitude

When the soul-star chakra is balanced, you feel and understand your purpose and can access memories of your past lives. When it is unbalanced or blocked, you feel restless and ungrounded.

Clear quartz – This is the most powerful healing and energy/thought amplifier and can amplify the energetics of any other crystals it is near as well. Clear quartz enhances psychic ability to the highest level possible and attunes you to your spiritual purpose. When using clear quartz in meditation, it filters out distractions and is the most efficient in reprogramming. Being the powerhouse master healer that it is, clear quartz can stimulate the immune system and bring balance back to the body.

Selenite – This unique crystal can self-cleanse and recharge itself. Selenite clears, opens and activates the third-eye and crown chakras to help you reach your higher self during meditation and spiritual work. During these meditations, you can break down negativity and reveal truths to yourself. Selenite promotes honesty, purity and peace and aids in healing, balancing and stabilising the emotional body. Selenite is also used for good luck and protection.

Placement: above the soul-star chakra – about 12–18 inches above your head
Colour: white
Meaning: this is your communication with Source, spirit guides and angels – your spiritual connection and how you receive messages and synchronicities
Crystals to use: lodolite, spirit quartz
Message: be open to receiving with no pressure

When the spirit chakra is balanced and open, you are able to receive messages and see/feel synchronicities all around you and link into the spirit realm. When it is unbalanced or blocked, you can prohibit the messages from coming through.

Lodolite – This is an incredible tool to use during meditation, as it brings along big energy and vibrations which enhance your manifestations. Lodolite is said to be a window into another world and can also cause a cosmic shift in consciousness. Lodolite is also known as the shaman's crystal, as it allows you to recall knowledge of your past lives and enhances communication between you and your spirit guides. During these journeys, lodolite also provides protection, aids in releasing fears/blockages and promotes deep emotional healing. Lodolite is excellent for those who like to practise lucid dreaming and not only journey into past lives but on a cosmic level, a soul level and a personal level.

Spirit quartz – This is a crystal of harmony and alignment and is the bridge between you and your spiritual journey and path, as it has extremely powerful and high vibrational energies. Spirit quartz is able to continuously amplify its energy through each and every point presented on the stone, as it is an aggregator crystal. Spirit quartz assists in revitalising energies, cleanses and clears blockages in the spirit chakra, and elongates the effects of spiritual healing work. Use spirit quartz during meditation to link yourself with the higher realms, as it enhances psychic energies. White spirit quartz is the most powerful of all, as it activates, opens and connects to all the bodies' chakras.

CHAPTER 1

Placement: above the spirit chakra
Colour: pearlised white/opalescent
Meaning: represents universal flow, infinite creationism and manifestation abilities
Crystals to use: astrophyllite, Herkimer diamond
Message: we are all connected

When the universal chakra is balanced, you have the ability to create and manifest all your desires, living in true alignment with your highest self and soul. This also allows you access to interdimensional travel.

Astrophyllite – This crystal is your soul keeper, infusing you with light and allowing you to reconnect with your spirit and your higher self. Astrophyllite gives you the ability to make important changes that can move you along in your life path, so you can find your true purpose. Astrophyllite gives you the tools you need to look within yourself, to recognise the changes that need to be made. Astrophyllite works with all the chakras but enhances the connection between the third-eye and crown chakras to further activate your soul-star chakra through to your universal chakra, allowing white light to flow throughout your body. Astrophyllite also resonates with those who need help resolving past-life experiences and can activate a strong soul connection between your past and new relationships.

Herkimer diamond – Known as an attunement stone, the Herkimer diamond is used to attune people and environments. Herkimer diamonds typically have double terminated points (i.e. a single point at each end of the crystal), which allows energies to be received and given freely. Herkimer diamonds can open and activate your third-eye, crown chakra and universal chakras, allowing you to communicate with your higher self and your spirit guides. Herkimer diamonds are said to be able to heal your physical body of ailments and help begin the realignment of DNA and energy within your body. Herkimer diamonds not only heal your physical body, but your emotional body as well, by allowing you to see your true self and look past your fears.

CHAPTER 1

39

Placement: above the universal chakra

Colour: white with pink/orange

Meaning: you receive messages from Source, spirit guides and your higher self, and you raise your vibration and the vibration of the collective; not everyone can activate this chakra to its highest potential but if you are able to, you will be in direct communication with Source and ascended light beings, and Source and the ascended light beings can also speak through you

Crystals to use: apophyllite, rubellite

Message: you are the channel

Once the galactic chakra is opened, it does not close; however you will not always stay in the state of 5D consciousness as you are human by nature. A natural fluctuation between 3D, 4D and 5D is to be expected. You will receive new ideas and ways of thinking and it will be an awakening for your soul.

Apophyllite – This crystal helps you maintain a strong connection between your spiritual self and your physical self. Apophyllite also acts as a conductor for vibrations and energies because of its high-water content, and in being a conduit, apophyllite can correct imbalances in your energies and enhance your psychic and clairvoyant abilities when opening and activating your galactic chakra. With Jupiter once being the original ruler of Pisces, apophyllite honours the fluidity that is required of you when curiously seeking growth in the depths of the unknown and becoming a channel.

Rubellite – This stone has properties that enhance and enable emotional healing, evoking your compassion and universal love to calm you in times of duress, heartbreak and anxiety. Rubellite urges you to use your emotional intelligence to acknowledge not only your feelings, but to understand and empathise with the feelings of others, emphasising the importance of universal oneness and connectedness.

CHAPTER 1

41

Placement: above the galactic chakra
Colour: shimmering gold
Meaning: ascension and connection to the cosmic womb, Goddess, Divine Mother and Source.
Crystals to use: pyrite, citrine
Message: you are a gateway for divine light

Once the divine gateway chakra is opened, you are a part of the universal oneness – part of the divine. Your mission is to bring love and peace to Mother Earth and assist the collective in their awakening and ascension.

Pyrite – Pyrite is most commonly known for bringing prosperity, wealth and good luck; however, this crystal also emits healing frequencies to increase your vitality and bring harmony and balance to your human system. Pyrite is also a highly protective stone that shields its wearer from negative energies and prevents energy leakage within your aura. Being illuminated with pyrite's shimmering golden energy, you can gain a deeper connection to the divine.

Citrine – This crystal is golden yellow in colour and emits a radiating golden healing light that can strengthen your enthusiasm for life and the future. While using citrine in meditation, you are able to deepen your state of enlightenment, through the divine gateway chakra, while exuding an energy of warmth that brings a rush of mental clarity, allowing you to have a clear connection in the cosmic womb.

The meridians: tapping with crystals

The Emotional Freedom Technique or EFT is a form of acupressure that uses two of your fingertips to stimulate energy (meridian) points on your body. It is another way in which I use crystals for my own healing and that of my clients. I use a method channelled by my spirit guides, which involves using crystals and EFT tapping.

By tapping on meridian points, you can release stagnant energies and blockages that have built up in the body. Simultaneously, while tapping, you also repeat affirmations or mantras in acknowledgement of these built-up energies and your intent to release them. You can articulate a different affirmation, mantra or acknowledgement at each different meridian point or repeat one over through the entire process, whichever you feel called to do. For example, if you're feeling anxious or stressed, you can say, 'Even though I am feeling overwhelmed, I accept myself.'

If you aren't familiar with the meridian system, it stems from Traditional Chinese Medicine and is the pathway through which your life energy (life force) or qi flows through your body. There are twelve major or primary meridians which are divided into yin and yang groups and are linked to the major organs in your body. Think of meridian points as each being a train stop, where your qi hops on and off the platform to deliver this energy (qi) to all your major organs. Just like your chakra system, when energies become blocked, unbalanced or stagnant, ailments can begin to manifest in your physical body, so it is wise to ensure that you can clear a pathway for these energies to travel through with ease.

Personally, I do not like to speak while tapping. I like to use my favourite healing crystal – a beautiful chlorite point with a channel face. Instead of using two fingertips, I use the chlorite point to do the tapping on my meridian points. With the crystal's additional energies, it allows me to clear these blockages and stagnant energies much quicker and more effectively, and I also find it quite revitalising, for when you're tapping, you can begin to feel the crystal emit vibrations when touched against the skin. My spirit guides imparted this method to me because… for one, I'm not a traditional human; two, I am an absorber of all the energies; and three, to teach *you*, the collective. Being a crystal guardian, intuitive empath and reflector (by human design), you can basically call me a human sponge. For this reason, the crystal usage during tapping is *key* in helping me release what is not my own and what no longer serves me.

Whether you realise it or not, your emotional, spiritual and physical bodies are always absorbing energies from other people and your environment. This can be a lot to handle, especially when you're trying to deal with your own. So, whether you're an empath or not, a reflector or not – you still need to be aware of how to release when you have become built up with energies that aren't your own.

Grab your favourite crystal and let's dive into the eight meridian points you will be tapping along!

Introduction to the eight meridian points

Work through the meridian points starting from the top to the bottom, to the karate chop (number nine). **Repeat for as long as necessary until you feel you no longer need to continue this process.**

- Top and centre of your head
- Start of the eyebrow
- Side of the eye – on the bone
- Under the eye – on the bone
- Under the nose – centred and directly above the top lip
- Chin – directly under the bottom lip
- 1 inch under collarbone
- Under arm – in line with nipple
- Karate chop – outside of hand

Selecting your crystals

Many people ask me, '*How do I select a crystal?*' – to which I say, that decision is completely up to you! Some choose crystals simply for aesthetics, some choose by what emotions a crystal evokes within them, and others choose them by deciphering in what manner the crystals can amplify their healing. The lesson to take away here is that *there is no wrong way* to select crystals.

As many of you may have heard by this point, crystals choose you, you don't choose them. This is generally the way crystals come into my life, as I can feel my etheric body and soul calling out for what it needs, not only for my personal life, but for the collective and in my business as well. I will get a channelled feeling of energies for what the collective needs at any given time. For example, I will get a message that the collective is needing to practise more self-love, or that the collective needs to shift and practise deep healing on an old trauma or wounds to experience further growth on the journey that is ahead.

When you are selecting your crystals, there are a few things to take notice of as you begin to understand your soul is asking for them on a deep, authentic level:

What colour crystals are you drawn to?

- This can indicate which of your chakras are out of balance, overactive or need some extra attention. i.e. black, red, orange, green, blue, purple, pink, white etc.

What crystal shape are you selecting?

- The shape of the crystal is the way it emits its vibrational frequencies and can enhance your healings in a specific way. i.e. cluster, generator, sphere, tumbled stone.

What is your intended use for these crystals?

- Are you planning to use your crystals for home decoration, practising crystal healing or meditation?

After answering these questions, you can begin to document what areas of your etheric body you need to focus your attention on and what may require an energetic shift or healing.

Lastly, go by what you *feel*, because your intuition is the greatest gift you hold within you, and it will never lead you astray. These are the steps I take on every crystal selection journey.

Crystal shapes

There are so many different types of crystals and shapes, it can get quite overwhelming when you're looking to add to your collection or begin your healing journey. Be aware that a crystal's shape isn't purely for aesthetics; it is the way each crystal emits its energy and vibrational frequencies. Its shape can enhance the way you use the crystal; it can enhance its metaphysical properties and, based on where you place them, can define its purpose to work in perfect alignment with you, for you and for your environment.

On the next few pages, I'm going to go over the most prominent shapes, what these shapes look like and mean, where they can be placed in your environment, and how they can be used in your everyday life.

This is a larger crystal or point that is covered partially or completely in other smaller crystals. Aggregator crystals are a representation of the old soul (the larger base) working in conjunction with the new soul (the formations growing on the larger base). An example of an aggregator crystal is spirit quartz. Each new soul forming on the old soul also contains the power to project and amplify energies and intentions.

Aggregators are a crystal to bring unity; they are best used with large groups of people, the workplace and within your family. They can also bring unity and peace to your human system by unifying and balancing your chakra system when used during meditation and gridding on your body.

Brings unity and an amplification of energies.

CHAPTER 2

) CLUSTER (

This is a crystal with two or more points growing from the same crystalline matrix (base) in which each terminated point of the cluster will emit energy. Crystal clusters are a beautiful formation to keep around the home and office space, since clusters can radiate and emit energy through each terminated point in every direction. They are also able to absorb and transmute negative energy in your environment, to a higher, more positive unifying frequency.

Put your clusters near your other crystals to further amplify their natural properties as well. Additionally, since crystal clusters have so many terminated points, they can magnify the intentions you set and instil within them.

Energises and unifies your space,
and charges other crystals.

This type of crystal has a terminated point on both ends that have been grown from seed, not on a matrix, and these points can be natural or faceted/shaped to be this way. Since double terminated points don't have a base or bottom, energy flows through the crystal and emits energy and vibrations through each point, which means that they can both send *and* receive energy. Double terminated points are great to use while making crystal grids, for healing grids placed on the body and during meditation.

Sends and receives energy and information. Has the ability to transmute negative energies. A shape of balance.

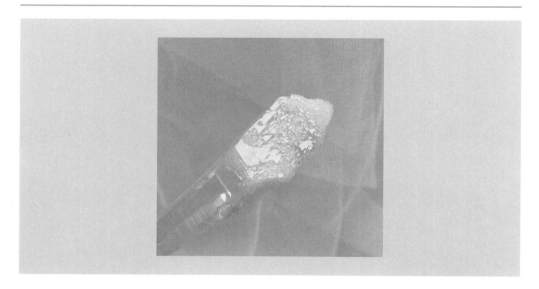

This type of crystal comes with many other names such as skeletal, alligator or jacare. The elestial shape appears to have etchings in geometric patterns, which is actually multiple triangular or pyramid-like shaped terminations forming over each other from the same base. You will find the elestial shape is some form of quartz – clear quartz or smoky quartz.

Elestial crystals are extremely powerful and carry high vibrational frequencies that can heal and cleanse the collective. Their geometric nature makes these elestial crystals a way to access sacred knowledge and to tap into the divine to receive guidance. Elestial crystals aid you in cleansing your emotional and etheric body by allowing you to clear blockages and remove old traumas and woundings you may have carried over from past lifetimes or created in this current lifetime.

Use elestial crystals in meditation and during crystal healings to reap the benefits. Keep these crystals in a sacred space or your altar space.

Emits high vibrational frequencies to accelerate deep cellular healing.

) GEODE (

This is a spherical or subspherical formation with a hollowed, internal cavity that contains separate minerals growing inside. Geodes generally have a thick outer layer which has allowed the internal cavity to survive tough weather conditions, allowing it to grow further.

Each geode formation is unique on its own and contains big, beautiful energy. Geodes are wonderful to place around the home as they have powerful absorption properties that can transform energies into healing and protective vibrations. I like to place geodes near the entry and doorways, and in corners of specific rooms like the family or living room and bedroom areas, as they can provide you with a barrier from the outside world.

Aids in deep cellular healing while emitting grounding vibrations.

Generators have a crystal point with a flat base and contain six-faceted sides meeting together at the tip – called the terminated point. Generators are one of my favourite shapes as they bring energy through their flat base and project it through their terminated point. This energy enhances and brings stable, grounding vibrations to any room, altar or sacred space they are placed in.

Use generators in the centre of crystal grids, during meditation and while doing crystal healing, as the energy can be aimed in the direction of your specification.

Six-faceted point that amplifies frequencies and self charges along with charging other crystals.

Heart-shaped crystals are a representation of pure divine love and have a deep emotional and spiritual connection to the heart chakra. They emit calming, peaceful and loving frequencies, and these frequencies are amplified when used during meditation by placing them on your heart chakra.

Heart-shaped crystals can also be used to deepen your love within yourself, but also to attract new romantic and platonic love interests.

Typically palm-sized, heart-shaped crystals can be carried along with you, or larger-sized statement pieces can be placed in the home and bedroom.

Emits the frequency of pure divine love.

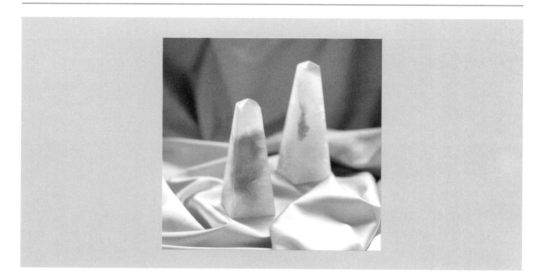

Obelisks have a four-faceted shape that tapers to the tip (also known as a pyramid apex). With a connection back to ancient Egypt, obelisks represent vitality, duality and balance, as well as being a representation of 'as above so below' – meaning what happens on one plane of reality is also occurring simultaneously on another.

Obelisks were made to dissipate a build-up of stagnant energies. They absorb the energy from the Earth, through the base, releasing it through the tip into the atmosphere, allowing it to circulate and create balance. Place obelisks where a heavy energy build-up is most common, i.e. the living room or office space.

Obelisks also hold abundant sacred knowledge that you can tap into. While in meditation, hold an obelisk upright in your left hand. Rub one of the four-faceted sides to allow your crystal to release the knowledge to you. Each facet of the obelisk will contain different information; you can add this process into your meditation practice.

Holds sacred knowledge that is ready to be released to you.

This crystal is oval in shape and polished, made to fit in the palm of your hand, and radiates energy in all directions. Palm stones have a particularly great grounding frequency that helps reduce stress and anxiety when you place them in the palm of your hand.

Palm stones are also the perfect portable size for you to keep on your person or in your purse for an extra layer of auric protection. You can also use palm stones during crystal healings, by placing on your chakra system, and to enhance meditations by putting you in a deeper state of relaxation to connect with higher frequencies.

Placing palm stones under your pillow while you sleep can also trigger deep cellular healing, providing you with a restful, full night's sleep full of calming and relaxing vibrations.

Has a grounding effect on your etheric body while reducing stress and anxiety.

These crystals are typically attached to the end of a metal chain or string, and they come in many shapes, both angular and round.

Pendulums are used for spiritual work, specifically self-growth and healing, and connect you to higher energies to locate and unblock unwanted energies. Pendulums help the user gain insight and guidance from Source by asking the pendulum a *yes* or *no* question. When suspended in the air, the pendulum will swing back and forth or in a circular motion (in whichever manner you have trained it to do so) indicating a 'yes', 'no', or 'maybe' response to a question you have asked. Once the pendulum has absorbed the energy, it will then come to a halt.

This technique of suspending the pendulum in the air is also used during healings to align and unblock your chakra system and balance your mind, body and spirit. Place the pendulum over each chakra; if the pendulum begins to move, then it is aligning a chakra that is unbalanced and inactive. Once the pendulum comes to a halt, the chakra has been realigned and opened. Continue to do this throughout the entire chakra system for maximum healing.

Connect with Source for guidance and
realign your chakra system.

☽ PYRAMID ☾

This is a four, triangular faceted shape with a square bottom base (also known as a pyramid apex). The base of the pyramid provides grounding energies while the triangular facets (making a point) act as an amplifier of energies – making them an energetically, well-balanced shape. Pyramids are also linked back to ancient Egypt and are a sacred geometry structure that has the innate power to enhance your manifestations and amplify your intentions out to the universe.

Pyramids are well placed in the centre of a crystal grid and in any room or sacred space, as they are able to balance the energetics of any room and restore balance when required. Pyramids, if a smaller size, can be placed on your third-eye chakra, allowing extra energy to come through this centre to connect deeper to Source.

Acts as a balanced, grounding crystal that also focuses and amplifies high frequency vibrations. To be used for manifestation and healing.

) SCEPTRE (

Sceptres form naturally with the base of the crystal around the central 'rod'. Linked back to the ancient civilisations of Atlantis and Lemuria, sceptres were used by the high priestesses and high priests for healings and ceremonies. The sceptre is a symbol of great power as it can generate, amplify and transmit the highest frequencies with intentional direction. You can focus their vibrations and frequencies on healing and removing blockages from your physical, emotional and etheric bodies.

Sceptres allow you to claim back your personal power and align your soul journey with your human experience, aiding you to live your most authentic life. When working with sceptres, you can overcome your struggles with procrastination and live within your creative mind once more. Sceptres can also align, open and activate your entire chakra system, making connection with your higher self and the divine seamless.

Sceptres can be held with intention and used during meditation to reach a deeper transcendental state. When not in use, place them in your sacred space or on your altar.

Increases your connection to the divine while emitting high frequencies for alignment.

) SPHERE) (

These crystals have a spherical shape that emits and radiates the energy of their entire surface space. This energy is generally one of harmony and positivity and would be well placed in your home or office space.

Using a crystal sphere is also a way to enhance your healings or meditations, since they are circular, giving access to the cyclical properties of past, present and future and allowing the healing of generational, karmic and past-life wounding and remembrance. Crystal spheres also allow for an uninterrupted flow of energy that can aid in balancing and grounding the surrounding environment.

Spheres are also commonly used for scrying and enhancing psychic development.

Emits harmonic frequencies evenly from all directions.

These stones are formed from small, raw pieces of any type of crystal that has been tumbled and polished to create a smooth surface. Generally, the shape is irregular and varied in size, but don't let the size deter you as they pack a big punch. Tumbled stones, due to their shape, are able to radiate energy in all directions. They are easily carried in your pocket, purse or pouch, and are wonderful to use in creating crystal grids on surfaces and on your body for healings.

Radiates gentle, even energies from all directions.

Hand-carved into shape from their natural form, crystal wands date back to the ancient time of Atlantis where they were used by healers. Similarly, today, wands are a powerful healing tool used by healers and shamans alike, as they absorb universal energy and transmit these energies directly through their tip.

Wands are wonderful to use on your entire physical body, as well as when you need to direct healing on specific points on your etheric body and chakra system. Wands will scan your chakra system and your aura, homing in on any blockages in your chakras and repairing leakages within your aura. This ensures you're left with an energy system that is flowing freely with white light energy.

Wands contain energy that is focused, direct and grounding.

CHAPTER 2

65

Crystal formations and inclusions

Not only is the shape of a crystal important, but some crystals will also contain different formations (within these shapes) and inclusions as well. These formations and inclusions carry additional properties and energies that are an extra boost to your already shaped or natural crystal when it comes to your healing and usage.

Otherwise known as Lemurian lines, Akashic lines will typically be found on Lemurian seed crystals. They are horizontal lines that feel as if they are etched on some facets or all facets of the crystal. These lines contain sacred information within each line left by the ancient Lemurians.

To access this sacred information, use Lemurian seeds during meditation, by placing the crystal in your right hand, and moving your thumbnail on the etchings along the side, starting at the bottom and reaching the top etching to attune into the presence of your spirit guides and ancients. They will assist you in tapping into your intuitive energy and help you deal with complex situations and issues you may be encountering.

Access sacred knowledge from the ancient Lemurians and promote deep healing.

CHAPTER 2

A bridged crystal has a smaller crystal growing from the main body or matrix, offering an extra boost of energy to the main crystal body. Use these crystals during meditation, holding the crystal by the bridged point, to activate these additional energies.

Boosts the existing energies of the crystal.

These crystals contain a larger seven-sided face with three smaller triangular faces on either side, and with another triangular face directly opposite the seven-sided face. Channelling crystals allow you to channel messages and energy from Source, your guides and the divine light council, as well as the energy embedded in these crystals.

These messages are here to help you clear blockages, heal old wounding and trauma embedded within your human system, and receive guidance when called upon. Channelling crystals help enhance your intuition as well, when used in meditation.

Receive healing messages and guidance
from these crystals and Source.

This is a diamond-shaped window on an existing faceted point – also known as a sixth and seventh face. A diamond window will be sitting at the top of the crystal face which is connected by two leading lines – one that goes straight down to the base and one that goes towards the tip of the apex or termination.

Diamond windows are used as a portal to see deeper into yourself and your soul. They show you the truest, authentic version of yourself, so you can align with your highest self and live according to your soul mission. Diamond windows allow you to make the changes in order to be in pure alignment and let go of what is no longer serving you.

A portal into your soul.

This is a hexagonal shape that is recessed in the crystal near its base. Key crystals are used to dive deeper into your spirituality and awaken and activate sacred knowledge that is embedded in your DNA. With these activations, you will be able to access hidden or lost parts of your self and soul that you can once again awaken to. Look to key crystals to ask questions and receive answers – they are here to assist you on your life's journey.

Receive and unlock activations and guidance.

Occurring when other minerals are suspended inside a crystal, inclusions can be all sizes and colours and may appear as spots – they can even take up most of the crystal. For example, a crystal that is named after its inclusions is lodolite, which means 'muddy stone'.

Inclusions enhance the properties of the mineral it is inside, and but also projects the metaphysical properties it has itself as a mineral. The colours of the inclusions will also not only correlate to your chakra system, but they contain the power to amplify all of your manifestations, desires and help you discover your soul path and mission in this lifetime.

Enhances the mineral it is inside and amplifies
your manifestations and desires.

This crystal has a primary face consisting of five sides with a tall point at the top – forming a pentagon. Named after the ancient Egyptian goddess Isis, these crystals have a strong connection to the divine feminine and goddess energy.

The Isis face is extremely powerful, but also emits a gentle, nurturing energy and is considered one of the most efficient healers when it comes to your emotional body. The Isis window can also harness the elemental energies of earth, wind, water and fire, making your healings and meditations balanced and leaving you with a sense of stability.

Connect with the Goddess energy to promote healing and a balanced emotional body.

CHAPTER 2

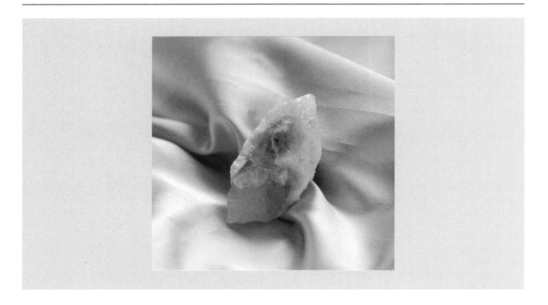

These crystals have a coating layer over the main surface area, which is generally a white, light grey or opaque colour and can be felt if you run your hands over the crystal. These coatings can sometimes have inclusions as well and are typically comprised of chlorite and other silicate minerals.

An overcoat adds powerful yet soft, nurturing energies to the crystal it is coated on. These coatings give you the courage and confidence to help you take your power back when you are feeling unheard or controlled.

Take back your power.

Known as a ghost or shadow crystal, this occurs when a crystal has stopped in its formation process and another mineral has started growing on it. When the original crystal begins growing again, it is layered with both minerals and takes on a 3D effect of the crystal within a crystal. The phantom will also take on the same shape as the original crystal and can have more than one phantom inside. Phantoms contain the energies of both the original crystal and the phantom inclusion.

Phantom crystals are a way to connect to your spirit guides, higher self and Source, as well as to connect deeper into your spiritual practice. Due to the way phantom crystals have formed, they contain a specific frequency of personal evolution and growth – which can help you move through any up-levelling and transitional periods you may be facing. By using phantom crystals in meditation, you can also connect with your past lives and clear any karmic contracts that may be lingering.

Experience your own evolution and growth by connecting with Source and clearing karmic contracts.

☽ RAINBOW ☾

These formations occur when there is a fracture within a crystal which displays itself as a prismatic rainbow. They can be visible to the naked eye or when reflected with light.

Rainbows will elevate the overall vibration of the crystal it is within and bring an overwhelming sense of joy, helping you combat negative feelings and energies. Rainbows will also help you heal, open and activate your entire chakra system, bringing you balance and helping to prevent energy leakage through your aura.

Elevate your vibration and heal your entire chakra system.

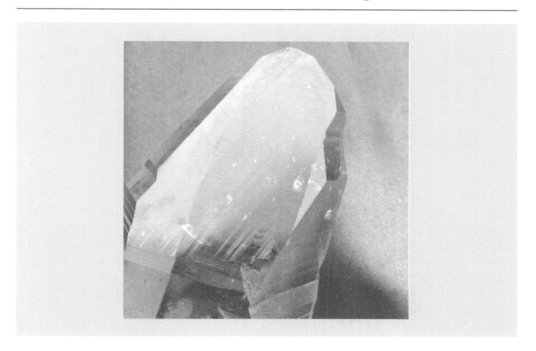

These crystals have one or more triangular indentations visible on a face, which can sometimes be a raised triangular shape facing upwards or sideways. Record keeper crystals are fairly rare.

A raised record keeper is a way to access your past lives and the lessons you learned. A sunken record keeper is a way to access programmed information from the ancient Egyptians and Atlanteans when used in meditation.

Access sacred knowledge from the ancients and your past lives.

These crystals have golden yellow or reddish-brown hair or needle-like inclusions, varying in size and thickness. Each rutilated quartz is different and unique.

They are extremely strong energy amplifiers because they combine quartz (which is a master healer) and rutile inclusions. Use these points to assist in manifestations and stimulate spiritual creativity, as rutilated quartz will blast your thoughts and intentions into the universe. With these powerful, amplified vibrations and energies, you will gain access to your divine, higher self and deepen your psychic gifts.

Rutilated quartz can also assist in clearing blockages in all chakras while simultaneously providing you with mental clarity and the concentration you need to set yourself on the direction you desire.

Amplify your manifestations and tap into your higher consciousness.

These crystals have been broken at the matrix or a termination and have begun to seal with new regrowth at these points. This can be caused during formation due to the Earth's natural movements. Self-healed crystals will regrow crystalline layers that can appear like scales or triangular layers (like elestial quartz).

Self-healed crystals are wonderful to use on your own healing, as they can bring up old behavioural patterns or past-life trauma you have repressed, in order to acknowledge them and release them to allow for further growth emotionally and spiritually. They will do this while sending you gentle reminders to stay persistent on your journey and that you can work through anything you set your mind to.

Release old behavioural patterns and past-life
trauma to grow emotionally and spiritually.

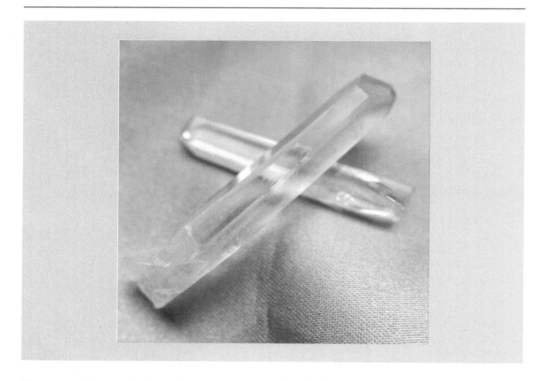

These crystals contain long clear quartz points that look like long seeds or laser wands and give off a melodic note/tune when they are touched together. Singing quartz are high-pitched, extremely high vibrational crystals that emit this energy on all frequencies and can send you into a deep, transcendental state when used in meditation. Singing quartz also has deep ties with galactic energies, connecting you to your spirit guides to receive guidance and clarity from the questions you seek answers to.

Connect with galactic energies and spirit guides to gain clarity and guidance.

Time link crystals have a long four-sided, rectangular facet that looks like a slanted diamond shape on a termination. Time link past crystals will have the window facet slanted backward. These crystals are a representation of your past lives, from which you can access information to help you on this current timeline. When using time link past crystals in meditation, you can access your Akashic records and messages from your soul book that will offer you guidance on how to break and release old behavioural patterns and energies stored in your emotional body that no longer serve you.

Initiate and undergo healing to experience growth.

CHAPTER 2

These crystals also have a long four-sided, rectangular facet that looks like a slanted diamond shape on a termination, but the window facet is slanted forward. These crystals will exhibit your future possibilities. When in meditation with time link future crystals, you can travel to possible future realities to help you make the choices that align with your soul purpose and serve your highest good. Always remember, the future is not set in stone, as the outcomes are constantly changing with every decision that you make. Use time link future crystals when you feel undecided or uncertain and need to gain some clarity. These crystals also act as a manifestation amplifier, so speak to these crystals with clear intent.

Weigh out your possible future reality
and manifest your outcomes.

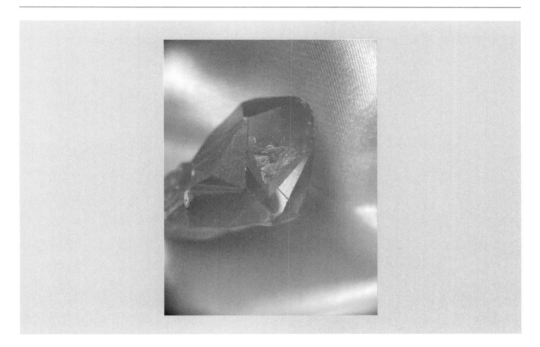

Another form of record keeper is the trigonic record keeper, in which the triangular formations are pointing downwards. Trigonic record keepers help you reach the higher realms, remove negative energies and entities, and aid in healing your etheric body. Trigonic record keepers are also helpful in recovering your soul purpose.

Access the higher realms and accelerate healing.

This crystal has two points adjoined together by their faceted sides from the one base. They are typically around the same height and grow parallel to one another from the base.

Twinned crystals are a representation of yin yang energy – the balance between the masculine and feminine. They are wonderful for working on your relationships, platonic and romantic alike, as twinned crystals teach you how to stay in the space and frequency of harmony and accord.

Balanced flow of masculine and feminine
energies. Emits harmonic frequencies.

Cleansing your crystals

Cleansing your crystals is vital if you are working with their energies on a daily or frequent basis. When you use your crystals for healing, or even if they have just been sitting stationary for some time, they build up with energies that need to be released – much like your own human system can build up energies. Cleansing your crystals restores them back to their true vibrational frequency, allowing them to operate at hundred-percent capacity.

To be kind to Gaia, please only use natural forms of running water such as a river, stream or a lake. If you do not have this readily available to you, there are other methods that are just as suitable for cleansing. Only use this method with crystals that are scored a five and above on the Mohs hardness scale – meaning no soft or porous crystals allowed! If you place a crystal softer than a five in water, it can begin to disintegrate, deteriorate and change its natural properties. Some examples of soft crystals to avoid in this modality are selenite, kyanite, calcite, fluorite, halite etc. Hard crystals include quartz and most forms of jasper. If you are unsure if your crystal can touch water, please make sure to do your research!

This modality can actually cleanse and charge your crystals at the same time due to the flowing nature of the water.

Tools required:
- Fine mesh bag
- Natural running water source

How to:
- Place your crystals in a fine mesh bag.
- While holding onto the mesh bag, safely place it in the river, stream or lake and allow the running water to wash over the crystals. If there is a location where you can safely submerge the crystals, you can do this as well.
- Allow the crystals to bathe for as long as you feel is necessary for their cleansing.

Do not use this method with crystals that are soft, porous or contain metal, as they can begin to disintegrate, deteriorate and change their natural properties. If natural saltwater is unavailable, you can add cooking salt to your water source. Remember to do your research first before placing any of your crystals in saltwater. Examples of crystals to avoid in this modality: opals, pyrite, hematite etc.

Tools required:
- Saltwater or cooking salt
- Ceramic or glass bowl
- Access to additional cool running water

How to:
- Gather natural saltwater – if natural saltwater is unavailable, you can add cooking salt to your water source.
- Place your crystals in a ceramic or glass bowl (no metal).
- Pour the water into the bowl, submerging the crystals and allow them to bathe for up to 24 hours – whatever you feel is necessary for their cleansing.
- When you are ready to remove the crystals from their salt bath, run them under cool water, ensuring you have rinsed any and all salt residue from them.
- Discard the remaining saltwater in the bowl, as it cannot be reused due to its collection of negative and unwanted energies.
- *Bonus tip – collect this water and place it in a windowsill or outside under the new moon or during the full moon lunation period, to give your crystals an extra boost of energy.*

☽ MODALITY: DRY SALT IMMERSION ☾

Do not use this method with crystals that are soft, porous or contain metal, as they can begin to disintegrate, deteriorate and change their natural properties. Use cooking salt or sea salt. Remember to do your research first before placing any of your crystals in salt.

Tools required:

- Cooking salt or sea salt
- Ceramic or glass bowl
- Access to additional cool running water

How to:

- Place your crystals in a ceramic or glass bowl (no metal).
- Fill the bowl with cooking salt or sea salt, submerge the crystals and allow them to bathe for up to 24 hours – whatever you feel is necessary for their cleansing.
- When you are ready to remove the crystals from their salt bath, run them under cool water, ensuring you have rinsed any and all salt residue from them.
- Discard the remaining salt in the bowl as it cannot be reused due to its collection of negative and unwanted energies.

Smudging is an ancient ceremonial ritual when you burn sacred herbs or resins to cleanse and purify your energy and environment. There are many tools you can use for smudging, including incense sticks, smudge sticks, ethically sourced palo santo, feathers or smoke-less smudge spray with essential oils. Some herbs and oils you can use for smudging your crystals include sage, cedarwood, lemon, sandalwood, lavender, sweetgrass, frankincense, myrrh and palo santo.

Note: I ethically source all of my herbs, oils, palo santo and feathers only through fair trade and what is available without harming Mother Earth. Find a reputable supplier and shop you trust that aligns with your ethics.

Tools required:

- Smudge stick, incense stick, palo santo, feather or smoke-less spray – use what you prefer
- Abalone shell or any shell that you have available and a glass or ceramic bowl to catch the debris from your burning smudge stick
- Lighter

How to:

- Light your smudge stick, incense stick or palo santo and hold your shell or bowl underneath your smudging modality of choice.
- Wave and waft the smoke over your crystals and let the smoke linger around them; this process doesn't take long as the smoke does all the work for you!
- If you choose to use a feather, just wave the feather in a sweeping motion around the crystals.
- If you choose to use a smoke-less spray, simply spray the environment around the crystals, and if the crystals rate hard enough on the Mohs hardness scale, you can spray them directly as well. NOTE: ensure that your crystals can handle the water and essential oils.

CHAPTER 3

Some crystals have extremely high vibrations, absorb less energy than others and can transmute negative energies. Some would call them self-cleansing, meaning they are great for boosting and cleansing the energies of other crystals.

The most common self-cleansing crystals are selenite, carnelian, citrine, halite and kyanite. Even though these crystals have this self-cleansing capability, they can still do with a good clean every now and again, since they are made up of energy and frequencies (as all crystals are). After all, we can all use a bit of tuning up sometimes.

This self-cleansing theory has become more prevalent in recent times as selenite, carnelian, citrine, halite and kyanite are said to transmute negative energies. However, there are many other crystals with this same capability, such as amethyst, quartz, chalcedony and so on. They are not described as self-cleansing, but I still like to use them for proximity cleansings, since they can transmute negative energies.

How to:

- Place the crystals you would like to proximity cleanse near amethyst, quartz, chalcedony, carnelian, citrine, halite, kyanite or selenite and leave them there for 24 to 48 hours – and that's it!

- Another fun tip is to always leave them stationed (when not in use for healings or meditations) next to a piece of one of these crystals, so it's always on top of its cleansing game.

CHAPTER 4:

Charging your crystals

After your crystals have been sufficiently cleansed, you can then charge them – the renewal stage. Charging your crystals is a way to set your intentions and work in unison with the stone. This will align the crystal's metaphysical properties with your energetic centres, allowing you to raise your vibration and access their higher healing powers, but also to embed the crystals with additional positive vibrations and energetic frequencies. This is when you are able to share your energies with one another.

I like to think of charging my crystals as blessing them and allowing them to reach their highest potential, as they are able to absorb additional, powerful energies that the universe is providing that might not be visible to the naked eye. Charging your crystals also provides you with a longer duration of usage (dependant on type of usage), but some of these methods will cleanse and charge your crystals fulfilling both seamlessly. Again, I want to urge you to use whichever charging modality you find fits best into your life, schedule and routine, and is energetically in tune with how you work with your crystals.

If you're having trouble understanding the difference between cleansing and charging, here is a handy reminder:

Cleansing crystals – to remove and purify
Charging crystals – to renew the energetics

My go-to charging modality is using sunlight and moonlight, as it is effortless, especially when you have a busy schedule. Sunlight is a strong, masculine energy that gives you an accelerated push forward. When you're looking for a vibrant, strong energy infusion, I recommend using sunlight as your charging modality.

Be sure that the crystals you are charging under these rays aren't photosensitive, as it can cause the crystals to fade or discolour.

How to:
- Place your crystals in an area where the sun can radiate onto them. This can be outside on a porch or deck, or if you don't have access to an outdoor area or simply prefer to keep a watchful eye out for your crystals, place them on a windowsill.
- Keep charging them under the sunlight for around 1 to 2 hours – that's always felt like the sweet spot for me and my crystals.

☽ MODALITY: MOONLIGHT ☾

You can charge your crystals under any lunar phase, as each phase contains different types of energies. The most common lunar phases to cleanse under are the new moon and the full moon – however, I also like to charge my crystals under the dark moon, as I resonate deeply with this lunar phase.

The new moon contains the energy of new beginnings, and this is the lunar phase where you want to set your intentions and plant your seeds for your manifestations. The full moon contains the energy of release and completion and signifies the finish of a cycle. This is the lunar phase where you can see the intentions and manifestations you set in the new moon phase blossom and come to fruition.

The dark moon is the end of the previous moon cycle and is connected to Goddess energy. The dark moon is where we take pause and recognise how far we have come and what further strides we can take to improve and grow further. It is a time for great introspection. Either way, in any phase you select, you gain gentle, nurturing and divine feminine energy added to your crystals.

How to:

- Place your crystals underneath the moonlight. This can be outside on a porch or deck, or if you don't have access to an outdoor area or simply prefer to keep a watchful eye out for your crystals, place them on a windowsill.
- Let your crystals sit there overnight.

☽ MODALITY: EARTHING ☾

Earthing is a method I like to use when I require a lot of grounding energies and to return my body back to stasis, and I like to use this method on crystals as well. Earthing your crystals means to return them to Mother Earth, by burying them in the dirt.

This modality is extremely potent when you have a crystal that is energetically heavy and overrun or that requires a deep cleanse and charge before you can reprogram it. When you have a crystal that requires a deep purge and earthing, I recommend that you use your intuition and your relationship with that crystal to determine the length of time it requires being earthed.

How to:

- Find a spot where you feel comfortable digging – and that you can remember – and dig a space for your crystal to rest.
- Either place your crystal directly into the dirt or put the crystal in a wooden box and then place into the dirt.
- Cover this space with dirt.
- Mark this area with an item so you can come back and unearth your crystals when you feel they have finished charging.

Energy transference is a term I use to describe handling, cleansing and charging my crystals. It is when I use my own auric field and energy from within to set a specific intention for each and every crystal I handle. This modality is one that I have been gifted from many past lifetimes and by Source. It is my soul mission to work with these crystals and match them specifically with each person they are intended for.

Although our gifts are different from soul to soul, this method is one I always recommend highly, as it deepens your connection and bond with your intuition and your crystal.

How to:
- Pick up and hold the crystal in your hands.
- Close your eyes and take three deep breaths.
- Let the crystal soak in the energies that are being emitted from your palms.
- Alternatively, rub the crystal between your palms to complete the energy transference.

Sound moves through our airwaves and is comprised of frequencies or pitch. Frequencies are classified as the speed of the vibration, which determines the pitch of the sound. Now, there are specific frequencies that are ultra-beneficial and healing not only to our human bodies, but to our crystals as well. Frequencies affect us at a deep cellular level because it is the way our human system and cells communicate as they exchange information to another cell via a specific frequency. If a frequency is not communicating properly, then we can become ill; our human system doesn't function at its optimum level, and we become unbalanced.

The same can happen to our crystals – they can become unbalanced if they need a boost of renewal energy – enter your sound charging modality. These sound vibrations are able to release and reset the energy of the crystal without changing its structure at a molecular level. So, once you have done your sound charging, the crystal is able to return to its natural vibrational state.

There are a few ways you can charge your crystals with sound: bells, chanting, crystal/singing bowls, drumming, singing, tuning forks. The beauty of using sound is that you don't have to move any of your crystals to perform the charge.

You can use this modality on any and all crystals – they love the extra vibrational boost and they all can be charged at the same time!

How to:
- Simply chant or sing loud enough and/or use a bell, crystal/singing bowl, drum or tuning fork close enough to your crystal subjects and they will absorb the vibrations.
- This can be done for a few minutes to a few hours – if you're feeling into the sound you're producing, just go with the flow!

☽ MODALITY: BREATH ☾

Breath is our life force, as it provides us with the necessary oxygen we need to function. Practising deep breathing has also been shown to reduce anxiety and stress, and improve our immune response and mental clarity. With the power of our life-force breath, we can set specific intentions and charge our crystals.

How to:

- Station your crystals so you can access their surfaces easily.
- Breathe in deeply, allowing this breath to fill your tummy and be charged with your life force (just a few seconds will suffice).
- While this breath is being charged, begin to set your intentions for these crystals (i.e. how do you want them to assist you – with healing? Manifestation? Releasing trauma?)
- Once you feel you have charged this breath and have your intentions stationed in your mind, release this breath onto your crystals.
- If you don't have many crystals to charge and would prefer to charge them individually, do this process while holding each crystal. As you breathe your life force onto the stones, you will be able to feel them vibrate with their newly gained energies and intentions.

Visualisation is the basis for our manifestations. When you can see and think about something so clearly in your mind's eye, you are working towards bringing your needs, wants and desires into this physical plane. It's like sending the universe a text message saying meet me at x spot at x time with x in hand.

So, if we can stimulate our thoughts and minds with visualisation, why can't we stimulate our crystals into becoming more energetically aligned and higher vibrational? Well, good news is – you can!

A bonus with this charging modality is that it actually cleanses and charges your crystals at the same time and can be done with a large number of crystals in the vicinity.

How to:
- Close your eyes.
- Imagine a bright white light surrounding you and your crystals.
- Picture this light purifying your energy, the crystals' energy and surrounding environment.
- See the light cleansing and drawing out the stored negative energies and your crystals being rebalanced.
- Once you have completed this ritual, open your eyes and feel the renewal energy within you and your crystals.

Programming your crystals

Programming your crystals can be quite the controversial topic, as some people find it necessary to program them and others don't. Crystals contain certain molecular structures that make them amplifiers of energies, and each crystal emits its own vibrational frequency, not unlike our own thoughts, chakra system and emotional body. Each crystal also contains its own set of metaphysical properties that can be harnessed when you are able to access these energies and frequencies effectively and properly. So, in saying this, my stance is that I don't program my crystals, since they are already created and formed with a specific set of properties, energies and frequencies by Mother Earth herself!

Since I've never been one to go with the grain, I take a different approach when it comes to the programming of crystals. My first step is tuning in and aligning my etheric body into a crystal's energy and frequency. I let myself feel what emotions the crystal invokes within me and the type of energy that I feel within my human system; so really you could say the crystal is essentially *programming me.*

By allowing myself to open up to the crystal's energies, vibrations and frequencies, I can then move forward with the method in which I can use them for healing and how to harness their properties with further clear intent. So, next I'm going to teach you some methods in which you can program yourself to intentionally align with your crystals.

Allowing others to program your crystals

Personally, I don't want anyone else programming or setting intentions for my crystals, unless I specifically request a certain healer to do so – for example, programming the crystals with light language. I want the crystals I keep to be charged with my energetic signature and intentions. Sure, you can go through the cleansing, charging and reprogramming process, however I find this unnecessary, especially if you didn't require this service from the get-go.

Purchasing crystals that have already been programmed also takes away from the beautiful bonding and connection process you go through when you receive your new crystals, and this is an important way to feel into each other's frequencies. I also believe that purchasing already programmed crystals diminishes your own personal power. The message that you are giving to your crystal and your intuition is that you aren't capable of doing this process yourself, when I can assure you, you most certainly are capable. In fact, you are the most qualified person for the position since you and your crystals were drawn to each other not by happenstance. I urge you to not let fears or doubts creep in by thinking that you don't know what you're doing when it comes to programming, because creating this bond is about you and the crystal and no one else.

Crystal programming with the chakras

The other way I align myself with my crystals is by using what I already have available to me – the twelve-chakra system (see chapter 1). Again, this involves doing your research about the metaphysical properties of your crystals, but I also highly recommend using your intuition to feel into their energy and frequency.

- Enter your sacred space or find a space where you will be undisturbed and can lie down comfortably.
- Start by feeling into the vibrational energy that your crystal is emitting – you can also go by the colour of the crystal.
- Place your crystal on the related chakra point and allow your energies to meld.
- The duration of this process does not matter – it's completely up to your discretion. When you feel it is time, you can remove yourself from the space.

Expressing your gratitude

Once you have selected your modality and practised your programming, it is time to thank your crystals for working in alignment with you. Since we are working with not only the frequencies of your crystals but the energetics of the universe and your human system, we need to vibrationally spread our expression of gratitude. When we are calling in our needs, wants and desires, we need to show we are grateful for what we currently have, rather than focusing on lack. Working from a lack mentality will only breed more lack.

When we recognise what we already hold, whether physically, mentally or energetically, we give thanks and gratitude to the universe for providing. Once we are able to hold space for what we have, we can then call in our new intentions and manifestations. Gratitude is a powerful weapon and doesn't cost you much other than a few seconds of your time and, in the long run, can only enhance the way you live. If you're stuck, you can try some different methods of expression of gratitude.

VERBAL EXPRESSION

- I thank the *crystal* for its assistance in my healings or manifestations (you can get specific).
- I thank the *crystal* for acting and working in alignment with my highest good.
- I thank the *crystal* for coming along each healing journey we embark on together.

NON-VERBAL EXPRESSIONS OF GRATITUDE

- I feel *joy.*
- I imagine what this crystal is helping me call in to enhance my life, and how that feels once I receive it.

There is no incorrect way to express your gratitude; do what feels right and aligns with who you are authentically, down to your core and soul. The more you express your gratitude, the more ways you and your crystals can spread this vibration.

PART 2:

CRYSTALS AND THE LUNAR CYCLE

NEW MOON

New beginnings and preparing for change

Over many years of working with crystals, I have created my own personal process for healing and manifesting my intentions, harnessing the power of the lunar cycle. In the following chapters, starting with the new moon, I outline the rituals and processes I use to help these intentions come to fruition during each lunar cycle.

The new moon is the beginning of every lunar cycle, when we do not see the side of the moon that is illuminated by the sun. Meaning, Mother Earth is stationed opposite the moon and the moon is aligned with the sun. The new moon is deeply embedded into spiritual practice as it signifies 'new beginnings', and is a time where you can tap into and harness its potential and momentum when you're feeling stagnant or simply want to call in new desires. It is the most potent time to begin planting the seeds for your manifestations and watch them flourish and blossom. During the new moon phase, I like to use crystals that amplify energies, assist with manifestation and inspire creativity.

Crystals for the new moon

Rainbow moonstone – Also known as the stone of new beginnings, rainbow moonstone relieves emotional instability and stress while providing you with the inner strength to get over any hurdle that may come in your way. Rainbow moonstone sparks inspiration and brings success not only in business affairs, but in your love life and relationships as well. With Mother Moon on your side, good luck and fortune will be right there to follow.

Rose quartz – Known as the love stone, rose quartz holds the energetic frequencies of deep, divine unconditional love. It can open, activate and balance your heart chakra, and when your heart chakra is open you vibrate at a higher frequency – calling in all that you desire. These vibrations allow you to remove blocks and self-limiting beliefs so you can manifest at your highest potential.

Indigo gabbro jasper – Both an amplification stone and a grounding stone, this makes indigo gabbro jasper a highly sought-after spiritual tool. This crystal allows you to bring forth your spirituality into the physical plane to continue your journey on your spiritual path. Indigo gabbro jasper works on an emotional, spiritual and mental level, aiding you to find balance. Indigo gabbro jasper wants you to accept the parts of yourself that you find negative, and instead of drawing negativity to the things you want to change about yourself, it helps you find ways to accept and love these parts. Indigo gabbro jasper has strong energetic vibrations but is very well balanced with masculine and feminine. Since it's so well balanced, it also helps meld together our past with the present, helping us face our past issues in order to be more in touch with our present situations and allowing us to manifest on a deeper level.

Green aventurine – Known as the stone of opportunity, green aventurine aligns your energies and intentions in a way that attracts wealth, success, good luck and of course opportunity. Providing insight to bring forth luck simply through pure determination and will for it to be so, green aventurine helps you set a positive mindset and shows you your self-worth, so you can begin attracting success and opportunities. This crystal wants you to live in your truth, and in doing so, helps you to clear any emotional blockages that have been stopping you from prospering. Green aventurine works on the universal system of what you put out, you will receive back. The lesson is to know your intentions, know your worth, know this is cyclical, and be conscious of what you're asking for and releasing.

Scolecite – When this high vibrational crystal is used in meditation, it helps you to connect deeper with Source. It also aids in dream recall and astral travel, and emits calming vibrations that allow you to reach inner peace and connection with your higher self.

New moon manifestation ritual

How to:

- Gather your new moon crystals or crystals that you feel aligned with energetically for promoting manifestation.
- Grab a journal and some loose-leaf sheets of blank paper and write down on individual scraps what you would like to manifest.
- Place each scrap of paper with a different crystal of your choosing and begin to make your connection with that specific crystal and its new intention. Hold it to your heart and repeat the words as many times as you feel necessary. Once this connection is made, keep the scrap of paper with the crystal until the full moon.
- When it is the full moon cycle, reflect in your journal on how you believe your manifestations came to fruition and in what form they have come into your life.

When the next new moon approaches, try this ritual and journal your observations. You will then see how your manifestations have entered your realm in physical form.

WAXING CRESCENT MOON
Setting intentions and making plans

During the waxing crescent moon phase, you will see a crescent illuminated on the right-hand side, laying almost directly in line with the Sun and Earth. Can you feel this energy building and exploding outward for the collective to feel and harness? The waxing crescent moon is a potent time to take the seeds you planted during the new moon and start making plans to see these seeds sprout into your tangible manifestations and visions by the end of the 28-day lunar cycle and what better way to harness this energy than by cleansing, charging and programming your crystals.

By harnessing the energies of the waxing crescent moon and infusing them into your crystalline beings, you will give your crystals a specific task and frequency to focus on to help you carry out your manifestations and visions. Cleansing, charging and programming your crystals is a beautiful thing to do during this phase every month.

Crystals for the waxing crescent moon

Three crystals that I like to work with during the waxing crescent moon phase are aquamarine, charoite and smoky amazonite. These three stones help target important chakras (throat, crown and heart) that help align me with my manifestation power. The ability to speak my truth with aquamarine allows me to live authentically. The ability to connect and open my crown helps me understand that I am being divinely guided by my spirit team and that they are here to bring me what I call for. Lastly, smoky amazonite allows the release of stress and anxiety, putting my system back to stasis in order to align to a more abundant frequency.

Aquamarine – This is an extremely powerful stone for self-healing and is my go-to for reducing stress and anxiety. With potent water energies, aquamarine's vibration will aid you in addressing any emotional insecurities, traumas and baggage that need to be cleared. Aquamarine also targets your throat chakra, allowing you to speak your truth and live your most authentic life. Reach for aquamarine when you want a wave of calm in the chaos.

Chariote – This rare and unique stone has a high vibrational energy and stimulates and energises the body, mind and spirit. Charoite shoots violet light through your crown and heart chakras, bringing high spiritual energy into union with unconditional love from the physical plane, and grounding it here on Earth where it is needed most.

Smoky amazonite – This crystal helps encourage you to be bold, speak your truth and aid you in attracting abundance. Smoky amazonite helps relieve stress and correct emotional issues and past traumas, while removing energetic blocks so you're able to have a clear mind when setting your intentions to attract abundance. This stone will also act as an energy filter to ensure your yin/yang are working harmoniously, allowing you to vibrationally align with the universe.

Ritual for setting intentions

Setting intentions is the age-old practice in which you clearly focus on an objective, desire or manifestation, and state how you intend to bring these into your physical plane of reality. It allows you to provide the universe and yourself with a direction in which you would like to move towards.

So, why is it important for me to set intentions with my crystals? Well, it is to harness and enhance not only the crystal's greatest potential, but yours as well. When you are crystal clear with your motives and desired outcomes, your human system begins to vibrate at a frequency to allow these objectives, desires and manifestations to make their way into your life and you are letting the universe know, 'Hey I'm ready to receive…!'

Here are some ritualistic ways to state your intent with your crystals…

Write down your intentions

How to:
- First, get together the crystal(s) you would like to set intentions for.
- Make sure to research the metaphysical properties of these crystals, so you can clearly align your intentions with their healing frequencies.
- Gather small pieces of paper and a pen – I like to use a black pen because the black ink can offer an extra layer of protection and cannot be erased.
- Write down your intention for each specific crystal, for example:
  'I want to attract abundance into my life.'
  'I want to heal my past trauma and wounding in my womb.'
  'I want to reduce my stress and anxiety.'
  (Don't feel boxed in by examples – allow your mind to roam free and dig deep into the path and journey you're currently on and where you would like it to take you).
- Fold the piece of paper and either wrap the piece of paper around the crystal or place it underneath its base.
- These intentions will remain with your crystals until you release them by cleansing and/or rewriting new intentions.

Verbalise your intentions

Following on from written intentions, I then like to take it a step further and speak these intentions aloud to the crystals. You can practice this any time that suits your lifestyle. I typically do this on a nightly basis, but particularly during this moon phase, depending on the type of intention I'm setting – for instance, when I was working on my deep trauma and sexual healing, I would speak these intentions nightly before I went to sleep. You can also practise speaking these intentions, even if you haven't written them down. I just find it adds extra potency by affirming what I want. Just like when you have your written intentions stationed with your crystals, your verbal intentions will also remain with your crystals until you release them via cleansing. You can either create new intentions or simply let the crystals act in accordance with the intent Mother Earth already has ingrained.

Visualise your intention – holding your crystal

Visualisation is another powerful technique to bring your intentions and manifestations to life and a harmonic addition to your crystals' existing energetics. Remember, before you begin this process you need to be ultra-clear on your intentions and outcomes, because if you have any fear around these intentions, you can manifest more fear and you will also vibrate at that frequency of fear, making the manifestation and intentions work in reverse.

I do this technique as I feel it is a powerful way for me to amplify and apply my intentions to my crystals. I like to do this one crystal at a time, because I want each crystal to hold individual, specific intentions.

How to:

- Begin by entering your sacred space or finding a space where you will be undisturbed and can sit down comfortably.
- Holding your crystal, with both hands, close your eyes and begin seeing with your mind's eye what you want to attract, achieve and manifest.
- Hold the vision clearly and tune into the following when you have attracted and received these intentions/manifestations: What does it *feel* like? What does it *look* like? What does it *sound* like?
- When you feel ready to leave this space and you have fully visualised what you want your crystal to help you attract, open your eyes. Your crystals will then hold these intentions and manifestations vibrationally within themselves.

Visualise your intention – third-eye projection

Your third eye is your connection with your psychic gifts and abilities, as it is your direct link with your gut intuition and inner knowing. Your third eye is also your gateway into other realms and planes of reality, which makes it an extremely powerful intention setting and manifestation tool. When we work in alignment with our third eye, we push our egos aside and can manifest and set intentions from the truest, most authentic space. In this space, we vibrate at a frequency of attraction, which we want when we work in unison with our crystals.

How to:

Repeat the process described in the previous section with these adjustments:

- Instead of sitting down, I recommend that you lie down comfortably.
- Instead of holding your crystal with both hands, place your crystal on your third eye (this placement is in between your brow area but slightly elevated towards the middle of your forehead).
- Hold your visions clearly and let your third-eye laser beam project them into the ether.
- When you feel ready to leave this space and that you have fully visualised what you want your crystal to help you attract, open your eyes.
- Your crystals will then hold these intentions and manifestations vibrationally within themselves.

CHAPTER 8

FIRST QUARTER MOON
Action and reflection

The first quarter moon means that the moon is a quarter of the way through the lunar cycle. This can be an integral time to see the intentions you set during the new moon start to form, and you may be feeling as if you're hitting some challenges or hiccups now along this journey. Just remember, don't allow yourself to feel defeated during this specific phase. You are being sent these tasks and challenges to see if you're truly open and ready to receive the manifestations you're asking for from the universe. This is your time to sit and meditate even more deeply, reflect on how you will make it through these challenges you're facing, and to take inspired action.

This time can feel stressful and bring about anxiety, so it is prudent to remain fluid in the decisions that you make and be gentle with yourself. Carve some time out to use your crystals to release any stress or anxiety you may be harbouring, so that when you are met with these bumps in the road, you can remain aligned with your visions and intentions from the new moon seeds you planted.

Crystals to reduce stress and anxiety

Being human, we can sometimes remain stuck in a 3D mentality which prohibits us from operating at our full potential. When stress and anxiety take over, your nervous system begins to shut down and you can begin to shut off from the world and others around you. I like to keep these crystals around to help keep stress at bay, but if it does rear itsugly head, I take a moment to harness the crystal's energetic vibrations in meditation, allowing my body to enter a state of relaxation, instead of flight mode.

Aragonite – This is classified as a star cluster, meaning it radiates and bursts energy and vibrations outward through all its points. Aragonite relieves stress, anger and emotional fatigue, while bringing vibrations of patience when you need it the most. However, aragonite is not for the faint of heart, as it will bring to the surface everything you are aiming to suppress – let it, and then work through it. This is how you truly become a master of your emotions and ultimately change the way you react to stress and anxiety.

Lithium quartz – This is used to activate and energise all your chakras but is specifically useful in opening and balancing your heart and crown chakras. When using lithium quartz during meditation, you can remove blockages, negative energies and attachments. Lithium quartz also allows you to simply relax and ease your worry, stress and anxiety, and with this relaxation comes harmony and balance restored to your body, mind, heart and spirit.

Kambaba jasper – This crystal brings a sense of peace and tranquillity and provides a calming effect on your mind, promotes inner peace, and offers powerful protection powers. Kambaba jasper also helps you understand your own personal needs and emotions, and guides you through changes in life and relationships, allowing you to approach these changes and situations with ease.

First quarter moon ritual meditation

Begin by gathering your crystals that assist you in reducing stress and anxiety. Lie down comfortably while holding these crystals in both of your hands or place them on your body where you feel you're holding the most tension. Begin to visualise how you see yourself, where you see yourself and how you feel when your manifestations come to fruition. Hold these visions with you and go back to them at any time. Your crystals will hold these visions and energetics within them and work overtime to align them with the universal flow, clearing blockages and aligning you with the frequencies of that which you desire.

WAXING GIBBOUS MOON

Making decisions and moving forward

Waxing gibbus moon phase is a time of great healing energy, encouraging you to look inward to see what you need to work on internally and emotionally. What are you willing to leave behind to move forward in your healing, expansion and ascension? What blockages need clearing? How are you able to better make ego-less, conscious, intuitive and soul-aligned decisions that will honour your higher self and highest good?

To get the crystal-clear answers from the universe, first you must clear your mind, and I mean really let your conscious mind take a back seat. I understand completely how this can seem like a daunting task, for I have an indecisive mind that goes a mile a minute, but that's why Mother Earth gave us the beautiful gift of crystalline energy to assist us, just as they did in realms and lifetimes past. We want to use these crystals to help us achieve mental clarity and also connect us deeply with our innate intuitive nature. Once we have come back to this connection, we can receive the guidance we have been searching for.

Crystals for mental clarity

Since mental clarity is sometimes hard to achieve in this fast-paced matrix we have created here on the Earth plane, you owe it to yourself to be able to shut off, look inward and reflect, without all the static floating around in your brain-space. When I find myself getting overwhelmed with environmental and social pressures, I know it's time to be still and clear the noise. These are my crystals to bring me ease of mind, focus and mental clarity, so I can re-centre and come back to a space where I am able to make informed and soul-aligned decisions and live again in alignment. Carry these crystals with you during the day and place them under your pillow at night for an extra boost of energetic clarity.

Bloodstone – This intense healing stone targets your heart, sacral and root chakras by cleansing and rebalancing your body. Bloodstone helps eliminate stress and anxiety by allowing loving energies to enter in, creating a constant flow of this vibrant energy throughout your entire body. Bloodstone firmly roots you to Mother Earth and helps resist negativity from entering your physical body and environmental spaces. Bloodstone is also known to enhance creativity and brings clarity and understanding to your mind and situations where there might be fogginess.

Optical calcite – This crystal is used to activate all your chakras, but primarily the crown chakra, and works by improving the flow of energy within your body, clearing any negativity in the way and allowing the positive energy to flow freely. If you're in need of clarity or need help ridding yourself of fear-based emotions, use your optical calcite during meditation and for manifestation. Since optical calcite removes these energy blocks, it will allow you to grow in your spiritual development. If you're seeking insight and clarity, optical calcite is what you're after.

Lapis lazuli – This is a powerful stone for creativity and strengthens clarity in thinking and communication. Lapis lazuli opens up your third-eye chakra to welcome in the wisdom of enlightenment and helps you arrive at your true spiritual destiny. When lapis lazuli activates your third-eye chakra, it allows you to access the deep knowledge that is embedded in your higher mind or consciousness, enabling you to be the ultimate truth seeker.

Ritual for mental clarity and decision making

It's time to raise your vibration and connect deeply with Spirit, for this is where your soul-aligned journey lies.

How to:
- Begin by finding a dark space where you will be uninterrupted, close your eyes and sit in complete silence for a few moments until you feel a grounding stillness invoked within. In this silence, we can connect deeper with ourselves and spirit.
- Once you have quieted your mind in this silence, grab a crystal for mental clarity and tap your third-eye three times with your crystal. This tapping will unblock and activate your pineal gland allowing your intuition to speak loud and clear.

CHAPTER 9

143

- After you have completed tapping, hold this crystal in your left hand, placing your right index finger on your mind's eye.
- If you're looking for clarity on a specific topic, now is the time to state the following affirmation: '*I see (insert topic) with the utmost clarity*.'
- Call upon your angels, guides and spirit for their guidance to offer you further insight into your situation.
- Your crystal will now hold this vibration of clarity on the topic you sought out and you can use this crystal in a grid, place it on an altar or carry it with you.

FULL MOON
Spiritual growth

The full moon is when the moon is fully illuminated from Mother Earth's perspective. Not only can you access the full moon's energy on the day she is fully illuminated, but these energies linger for three days prior and three days after. During this time you can release what is no longer in service for you and your energy. It is also a time to reflect back on what has come to pass and to give thanks and gratitude, as you would have gone through transformations leading up to this cycle.

Since the full moon is a representation of completion and carries a lot of big, sometimes heavy energies, it's important to work with emotionally supportive, protective, nurturing and healing crystals during this time, to keep you grounded and assist with your release. Through this release comes spiritual growth.

Crystals to increase connection with angels, spirit guides and the divine

Angels, spirit guides and the divine are always with you, and they have wisdom, knowledge and messages they try to get to you daily. They are here to guide you on your journey and help you reawaken to your own unique and special gifts that you are meant to share with the collective. These are a few crystals I like to use with the upper chakra centres during the full moon, to receive their messages and guidance more clearly.

Amphibole quartz – This rare form of quartz has inclusions of lithium to bring calmness, hematite to ground, kaolinite to relieve stress and limonite to aid in psychic protection. Amphibole quartz is here to provide a strong connection to your guardian angel and spirit guides to show you the path to find universal love and inner peace. Amphibole quartz also assists you in breaking out of your negative cycles and helps you to reach higher levels of consciousness.

Iolite – This crystal promotes introspection, allowing you to go on an inner journey with yourself to connect to your angels and your higher consciousness. Here to work with you on any past damage you're trying to heal from, iolite brings you peace along this journey of introspection. It urges you to take responsibility for your past actions and open up your communication to balance out your energy flow. The violet-blue energy that iolite emits, activates, opens and clears your third-eye chakra to connect you to the higher realms.

Fire and ice – Known as the stone of purification, fire and ice is a healing crystal that vibrates at a frequency that connects to all the physical and transpersonal chakras. Fire and ice cleanses, balances, opens and aligns all of your chakras with free-flowing, unhindered energy, allowing you to illuminate and open your consciousness to higher dimensions and dramatically increase your vibrational energy. Once opened to the higher dimensions, you may be able to receive wisdom and guidance to help with understanding your soul and its innate impulses. Fire and ice is here to align you with your true purpose.

Full moon ritual for seeking insight with divination tools

A great way to connect to your angels, spirit guides and the divine is with divination tools powered by your crystals. Grab a tarot and/or oracle deck, along with your crystals to enhance your intuition, and place the crystals on top of the deck(s). Then place both palms on top of the crystals and the deck(s), close your eyes and allow your energetic vibrations to align with those of the crystals and the deck(s). Begin by asking for guidance, either aloud or in your head, as to how you can achieve or move towards further spiritual growth and awakening. Conduct your reading in whichever manner you choose. Thank the deck(s) and your crystals for the guidance and wisdom they have imparted to you.

An extra step would to be journal the cards you have pulled, what they mean, what crystals you used and how you felt when you pulled these cards. You can keep track of these readings every full moon to track your progression.

Crystals to enhance your intuition and deepen your spirituality

Enhancing and trusting your intuition is a way of honouring your soul in past lifetimes, this lifetime and even moving forward through future timelines. These crystals allow me to deepen my connection with self, which in turn enables me to act in accordance with my highest self, my highest good, to live in the most authentic way possible for my soul and let go of what is not mine and what no longer serves me.

Tanzanite – Said to be a 'self-awakening' stone, tanzanite helps ignite your spirituality. Stimulating your throat, third-eye and crown chakras, it helps deepen the connection between your third-eye and heart chakras. When tanzanite activates this deep connection with the heart chakra, you will begin to experience yourself feeling and verbalising your unconscious truths. Tanzanite is also a great facilitator to enhance your intuition, and manifestation and psychic abilities. Radiating powerful positive energies, it helps to reduce feelings of anxiety and worry and instils emotional balance.

Seraphinite – Known as the stone of spiritual enlightenment and the stone of angels (seraphim angels), this crystal can play an integral part in connection for you too, allowing you to freely communicate with higher energies. Seraphinite is a great tool for self-healing and reaching higher planes of consciousness and assists you in breaking old habits, so you can focus on creating new, healthier patterns. Seraphinite also has a strong connection with the angelic realm, and by tapping into its vibrations, you can stay grounded while making your journey towards enlightenment and working towards the highest good. Seraphinite's green crystal energy, along with its silver-like swirls (angel wings), provides healing and rebalancing for the heart chakra.

Vesuvianite – Also known as idocrase, this is the stone of support and spiritual growth. Vesuvianite is here by your side to offer you encouragement and enthusiasm for life, while aiding you in exploring your spirituality and searching for your higher self. Offering healing and loving vibrations, it offers you information to understand your soul's purpose. Vesuvianite is used to align yourself with your true path and purpose, making it an excellent stone for healers.

Moon water – full moon ritual

A monthly ritual I never skip is making moon water during a full moon phase, to help me really sit deeply with my intuition and spiritual practices. Every full moon falls under a new astrological sign, which means each and every full moon offers something new energetically. I find this a potent technique – to bottle the energies of each full moon, helping me connect to myself on deeper level. Having this moon water in your arsenal will provide you multiple uses for months to come.

To create your full moon water, get your favourite container with a lid and fill it with drinkable water from a source that is readily available to you. Let the water be blessed by the moonlight (overnight) either in a safe space outside, near a window or on a windowsill. If the crystals you have selected are hard enough and will not be destroyed by water, you can also place them in the container with the water, allowing the moon and the crystals to supercharge it. If the crystals are not hard enough to be submerged in water, then you can create a circle around your moon water receptacle with these crystals and it will charge just the same.

You can use this moon water for other rituals, cleansing your other crystals or yourself via a bath, or it can be transferred into a spray bottle for spritzing on yourself or your environment when you want to harness some of Mother Moon's power.

WANING GIBBOUS MOON
Reflection and gratitude

The waning gibbous moon is a time to look inward, reflect and offer your gratitude. You have spent the last weeks tending to your seeds and visions, infusing your crystalline helpers with energies for a future soul-aligned path you wish to see yourself on at the end of the lunar cycle. Feel into this love and abundance you are sowing and spread that feeling to your loved ones and the collective by giving back – whether it be by lending a helping hand where it is needed or by offering your time in service to others… these are all the energetics of gratitude. Your expression of gratitude breeds more abundance, and so the beautiful, cyclical nature of gratitude will return to you tenfold.

Crystals to let go of fear around money and bring forth abundance

Abundance isn't only a tangible asset like money or material objects, it's a mindset. When we are able to recognise what we have – whether it be money and material possessions, or love and the company of partners, family or friends – we are able to call in more from the universe. To receive, we must be grateful for what we currently have, open and ready for what is to come, and vibrating at the same frequency as what we are calling in.

Yellow fluorite – This is the rarest of all the fluorite colours, and with its rarity comes big abundance energies and incredibly strong vibrations to enhance your manifesting. Yellow fluorite helps you focus so you can turn your goals and dreams into a reality; and its colour alone is a main attractor for abundance, wealth and prosperity. Yellow fluorite is also your beacon of clarity and calmness when you're in the midst of a chaotic situation, helping you focus your thoughts and bringing harmony to the situation.

Prehnite – This crystal deepens your trust in the universe by enhancing the Law of Attraction and allows you to feel certain that you will receive what you are manifesting. Prehnite also urges you to remain truest to your authentic self and encourages you to release any emotional baggage your body is holding on to. During this release, you will be able to move through blockages that are prohibiting you from calling in the abundance you desire.

Amazonite – This is the stone of truth and courage, encouraging you to be bold and speak your truth. In this truth, you are able to relieve stress, correct emotional issues and past traumas, as well as physical ailments. Amazonite will then bring in soothing energies to the home and workplace, acting as an energy filter and ensuring your yin and yang are working harmoniously. Being in this harmonious, energetic frequency allows abundance to flow freely to you.

Abundance ritual

How to:

- Grab a journal and start writing down the negative belief systems you may have about abundance/money that could be blocking you from calling in more.

- Now, below these negative belief systems you wrote down, practise gratitude by writing down the abundance that exists in your life currently. Write down what you have called in before that has materialised – a job, a place to live, a relationship etc.

- Once you have reflected on what the universe has provided in the past and present, write down three times, 'Thank you universe for always providing such abundance in my life'.

- Then it's time to create a gratitude altar by using your crystals. This doesn't have to be a large space; just place your abundance crystals and other items such as herbs, coins, candles and keys on it, to further enhance the energetics in a space where you can see it.
- Three days after you have completed this ritual, go back to your journal and begin reflecting on three things that have come into your life since you performed the ritual and created your abundant altar space.
- After you have reflected, write your gratitude to the universe again three times, 'Thank you universe for always providing such abundance in my life'.
- Continue to do this ritual for as long as you feel is necessary.

Crystals for removing blockages

Blockages within our etheric body system can have an adverse effect on our physical form. That is why I work daily with my crystals in meditation, yoga or any mindful practice that puts your human system at ease. When your etheric body is open, activated and can give and receive an energetic flow of light, that's when we are able to operate at our maximum potential. When we are not hindered by fear, doubt or physical ailments which stand in our way, that's when we can become our highest selves.

Flower agate – This healing stone radiates a soft, feminine energy that helps banish negativity and self-doubt, so you don't become your own worst enemy. By allowing this feminine energy in, you can restore balance to your qi and remove blockages that may be keeping you from blossoming into your highest potential.

Ruby in blue kyanite matrix – This is a powerful combination in one stone. Ruby and blue kyanite working together as one are here to keep you on your path to reach your highest good and protect you from any oncoming negativity that may be in your way. It helps to release old behavioural patterns that may also be acting as blockages and helps you stay nurtured and grounded, allowing positive vibrations to flow your way. Breaking the stone down into its parts, each brings its own properties to the mix. Ruby is a highly protective stone that also shows you the true value and nature of divine love. Ruby also helps you heal and become aware of your emotions, clearing any blockages in your heart chakra. Blue kyanite brings a sense of calmness and balance to the mind, body and spirit. Blue kyanite balances out the yin/yang energies and allows your qi to move freely throughout your physical body, without blockages.

Unakite jasper – This crystal helps to rid any negativity you may be holding onto from the past, whether it be from mistakes you have made or hurts you have experienced. Use unakite jasper during meditation to help release old blockages and to move through and forward with your emotional healing. Simply place unakite jasper on your third-eye, heart or sacral chakras while in meditation, to gain insight and wisdom on how to continue on your path of healing. Unakite jasper vibrates at a frequency harmonising love.

Moon water bath ritual

Remember that full moon water you made during the full moon phase? Now is the time to put it to good use. Water is such a powerful, metaphysical element, helping to clear blockages and nurturing your soul. With your full moon water, you will be able to clear the negative energies and blockages you're holding within your human system, your aura and surrounding environment.

How to:

- Begin by drawing your bath, adding any salts or herbs you enjoy; light some candles and have your crystals for removing blockages in tow.
- When you're ready to get into your bath, add your full moon water.
- While in this healing sacred space, begin by stating your intentions for removing blockages, i.e. 'I remove this programming and blockage from my mind's eye to help me...'
- Stay in this space for as long as you require and absorb these transformative and healing energies from your full moon water and crystals.
- When you're ready to leave, give gratitude for your healing experience.

LAST QUARTER MOON
Forgiveness and dealing with emotional baggage

The last quarter moon can be a somewhat tumultuous time to move through, as you are feeling the final effects of the full moon and heading into another new moon which can create some tensions internally. Old baggage, emotional wounding and ego can come forth to try and slow you down, but we won't let that happen. Acknowledge what has come forward and tweak your journey accordingly.

Start to question what in this suitcase of baggage isn't necessary for you to bring with you. Start to question what addictions or bad habits will not and do not serve your highest good and do not need to come along as a passenger in your next new moon journey. Habits are hard to break, that's why it's called a habit – it's habitual – and it's a ritual that doesn't help you reach your highest potential. We want to replace these habitual addictions or bad habits and raise your vibration. So, don't feel defeated or downtrodden during this phase or beat yourself up over the past – this is an opportunity for further growth and expansion. Instead, offer yourself the love, kindness and forgiveness you deserve.

Crystals for unconditional love

Unconditional love doesn't have to just represent a romantic partner; it's also the love you have for yourself. We all know by now, if you can't unconditionally love yourself, how can you love someone else fully, completely and truly? If you can't unconditionally love yourself, how do you expect someone else to? If you're having troubles making connections, platonically or romantically, it's time to check *within*.

These crystals offer the frequencies of unconditional, divine love – a love that may expose past trauma – but it is also a love that shows where you may be incapable of this love. The reason for this is so you can work on it, grow from it and learn from it – your shadow, that is. Our trauma and wounding doesn't have to stay with us forever. When we begin accepting and forgiving our shadow, we can begin to truly accept unconditional love from ourselves and others.

Pink amethyst – This crystal stimulates and opens the crown chakra, so you're able to act upon your intuition and allow yourself to be guided by your experiences. Pink amethyst allows you to fully align with, live in and own your soul's purpose and path, while radiating divine love, allowing you to accept yourself and others without judgement. Pink amethyst emphasises the energetic frequencies of healing, patience and love.

Ocean jasper – Known as the stone of joy, ocean jasper brings its calming and soothing water elements and delicate, soft healing colours. Ocean jasper promotes deep relaxation and urges you to reconnect to your inner spirit and Mother Earth's healing vibrations. Use ocean jasper during meditation to rejuvenate your spirit, be in a state of tranquillity and recharge your aura. Ocean jasper is a stone that helps you vibrate higher and in turn helps you reach a higher state of consciousness and unconditional love, as well as urging you to have a compassionate heart and to spread the love by connecting with Mother Earth. If you're having trouble confronting old emotional wounds and past trauma, keep ocean jasper with you to provide you with the strength to overcome your fear of facing these wounds. Ocean jasper is another great stone to use in deep introspection.

Strawberry quartz – This stone emits high vibrational energies to give you that energising and healing boost you've been looking for. Strawberry quartz contains all the properties of quartz with the powerhouse addition of amplifying your intention to seek universal love and balance. Strawberry quartz is a wonderful tool to use during your journeys, as it aids you in receiving knowledge that was once hidden and releasing any blockages that may be harboured within your heart chakra.

Mirror work ritual

Mirror work is a practice I use when I need to love myself more and feel more confident and self-assured. It's uncomfortable and confronting at the start, but it's a necessary step to self-acceptance and loving yourself unconditionally. When you're in a state of self-acceptance and unconditional love, you are able to offer these energies to your loved ones in return, and you will begin to feel your confidence rise in using your voice more authentically.

When you look into the mirror, you're going to immediately see all the thoughts and emotions you have about yourself reflected back to you, so this is where you can change those thoughts and emotions from being potentially damaging to uplifting and create a healthy relationship with yourself.

How to:

- Find a quiet space with your mirror so you are uninterrupted. If you don't have a mirror that is stationary in your space, just grab a handheld one or even use a compact.

- Gather your crystals for unconditional love and either hold them in your hands if that feels comfortable or create a circle around yourself with the crystals. This helps create a safe and loving energetic space for you to be held in.

- Begin to make direct eye contact with yourself; it may feel odd but let yourself feel through every emotion that is coming up and just experience it.

- Speak loving affirmations to yourself, while holding this eye contact, i.e. '*I love that I am...*' or '*I am enough*' or '*It's okay that I...*'

- When you feel ready, leave this space. Your crystals will hold the energetics of these new, loving affirmations. Carry these crystals with you daily and/or place them by your bedside to feel the full effects of their energetics.

- Repeat daily.

Crystals for clear communication

Your throat chakra is a vital component in communication – this is where we speak our truth, express our feelings and emotions and show our authentic selves to the world. If your throat chakra is blocked, not only will you offer poor communication to your peers, but you won't be fully in touch with your own intuitive guidance. However, when we fully align, activate and balance our throat chakra, we are able to fully express the wisdom imparted to us from our guides and higher selves. We all want to be heard and received without fear of persecution – so let's give ourselves and the collective the power to do so.

Larimar – This crystal works extremely well opening up the throat chakra to inspire better communication and release the energy and blockages you've been holding here. Larimar enhances any space by bringing in its loving energies and a sense of calm and serenity, which encourages healing. Larimar is also considered a seeker harmoniser crystal, which means that its crystalline energy structure aligns naturally to the power of the human mind, allowing you to speak from a place of true authenticity.

Blue calcite – Working to open and activate your throat chakra, blue calcite allows you to speak with conviction and communicate clearly. Blue calcite also activates your third-eye chakra, which can heighten your intuition and enhance your 'inner sight'. Place blue calcite under your pillow while sleeping to help you remember your dreams and the messages they hold for you.

Azurite – Commonly known as the stone of heaven, azurite is said to help in the pursuit of your 'heavenly' self. Native Americans used azurite as a sacred stone for communication with the spirit guides. Azurite is associated with the third-eye chakra and assists in awakening your psychic abilities. It can also be used with the throat chakra to help you recognise your intuition and remove energy/communication blockages and roadblocks in your progress. Azurite is a great tool to use during meditation to help clear your mind and allow you to go deep within yourself and receive intuitive messages clearly. Azurite also assists in relieving your phobias and negativity looming in your thoughts.

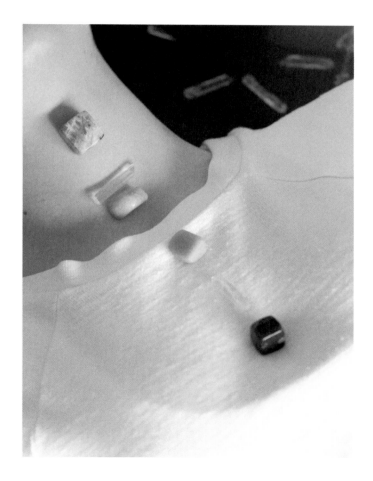

Ritual for clear communication

Blockages in your throat chakra can be caused by feelings of oppression and trauma and having been verbally abused in this lifetime and even past lifetimes. The clearing from this ritual can reach these blockages through multiple timelines.

Start this ritual by taking a crystal for clear communication in one hand, and gently rub your throat with it (ensuring you have chosen a smooth stone to avoid abrasions). Do this until you feel energised or a buzzing vibration. These energies and vibrations will begin to dissipate any blockages you may be feeling, allowing the bright white light within to flow effortlessly and freely through this centre.

Now it's time to turn on your favourite song and sing along, because there is no better way to heal your throat centre than by using it. Words are energy and power within themselves and by articulating them you are moving fresh, joyful energy through your system, further unblocking any residual remnants that may have remained. If you don't care to sing, then hum or whistle for the same effect. Repeat this daily until you feel like you're no longer holding back and are open to receiving.

CHAPTER 13

WANING CRESCENT MOON
Surrendering and letting go

Waning crescent moon is a time for great healing and surrendering to the flow of life. We will be headed into the new moon again and thinking of all the potential we can sow, but right now, it's time to focus on you, your life force and releasing any further resistances you may be holding onto in your physical and etheric forms. Offer yourself continuous emotional support and protection from that which does not serve your higher self.

Crystals for emotional support

Labradorite – Iridescent in nature and highly mystical, labradorite deflects negative, unwanted energies while providing a barrier to your aura to prevent energy leakage. It can help banish your fears and help you work through the insecure feelings you may be harbouring, allowing you to transform vibrationally, energetically and emotionally, while offering you a hand to hold through this process.

Peach moonstone – This crystal emits loving energies of the divine to every situation, as well as providing calming and nurturing vibrations. Peach moonstone raises your vibration and makes you more perceptive to the feminine energy within you and assists in soothing your worries and anxieties by reminding you of your own self-worth.

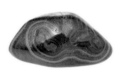

Malachite – Known as the stone of transformation, malachite helps protect you from negative energies by creating a strong energetic barrier around your person and absorbing these unwanted energies. In doing this, malachite promotes deep healing and positive transformations and, at times, may bring old emotions and past traumas to the surface to be dealt with in order for you to release and move forward.

Snowflake obsidian – Drawing emotions to the surface, this crystal can help you examine these emotions and potentially harmful thought patterns and behaviours. Since snowflake obsidian is the stone of purity, it also helps provides balance to your mind, body and spirit by allowing you to release what is no longer serving you energetically and emotionally while simultaneously providing you with mental clarity. Snowflake obsidian will also remove negativity from your person and your environment, helping to ease chaotic situations.

Kiwi jasper – Offering support in times of stress, Kiwi jasper also provides a sense of stability, tranquillity and wholeness. This crystal aligns all of your chakras and absorbs all negative and malicious energy that may be in your auric field. Kiwi jasper is a stone of healers, allowing you to heal yourself and aid in healing the collective.

Let it burn ritual

Remember those sheets of paper you wrote your manifestations on during the new moon that have been charged with your crystals and intentions? Well, grab those papers now – it's time to put them to use.

How to:

- Find a safe space, preferably outside *(only if you're allowed to burn off; I do not recommend doing this in a dry season),* though inside is fine too, near a sink and water. Grab a receptacle that is fire retardant and a lighter or matches.
- With your chosen crystals placed around you in a circle, light these pieces of paper and let their energetics be released into the ether. This will further solidify your manifestations from the new moon phase and assist you in releasing any blockages that would stand in the way of you receiving these gifts.
- Spread the ashes to the wind or bury them.

Crystals for protection

Protection from crystals can come in a variety of ways. They offer a shield of energetic frequencies around your aura to create a barrier between you and those who wish you ill or send negativity towards you. This shield can also act as a barrier for your aura to prevent your energy from leaking through, and it prevents energetic leeches/vampires (people who like to feed off your energy) leaving you depleted. Protective crystals can also absorb and sometimes even transmute negative energies in your environment or on your person into positive vibrations.

These are some crystals that offer this sort of protection and that I find are essential, especially for empaths, healers and lightworkers.

Obsidian – This is a powerful protection stone as it creates a shield around your aura to block negativity. Obsidian can absorb negative energies and deflect a psychic attack, while drawing out your mental stress and your tensions to clear and remove blockages from your psyche and aura. Obsidian is also a truth-enhancing stone – it allows you to speak your truth and confront yourself openly and honestly, so you can get to the root of who you truly are.

Black amethyst – This stone gets its colour from hematite inclusions within its crystalline matrix. Black amethyst enhances your intuition and your psychic abilities and provides you auric protection against psychic attacks and energy leakage. Black amethyst is a great stone for healers and empaths as it allows your body to rejuvenate, replenish and heal itself. It is also known to assist with migraines and headaches, as it aids in the removal of energy blockages stored in your third-eye and crown chakras, while simultaneously keeping you grounded.

Hematite – This highly protective stone helps absorb negative energies and transmutes them into positive vibrations. Hematite keeps you calm and grounded during stressful situations while offering a layer of protection. If you're doing deep spiritual work, hematite helps facilitate your connections to the higher realms, higher spiritual energies and the ascension process.

Ritual for crystal protection – create a crystal grid

For a boost of crystal protection for your person and environment, you can create a powerful protection crystal grid. If you have never heard of or made a crystal grid before, crystal gridding is essentially taking certain crystals and placing them in a sacred geometry shape to focus their energies on a specific intention and desired outcome. When you place all of these crystals together, they work in harmony to help you achieve this goal.

What you need:

- Any and all forms of protection crystals, as mentioned previously. I use a mix of tumbled stones and points, with a large crystal for the centre of the grid.
- Dried herbs such as bay leaf, star anise, lavender etc.
- A flat surface to create your grid on.

How to:

- Begin by setting your intention for this grid, i.e. 'I create this grid for protection for/from...'
- Evaluate your space and select a location where you would like to place your grid to receive its full effects, e.g. in a specific corner of your home or by a window to soak in the lunar and solar energies that will wash over your grid.
- What kind of shape would you like to make your grid? I always end up making a grid in a circular shape which I find incredibly powerful.
- Place your largest crystal in the centre of your grid.
- Working in quadrants of four, place a crystal in each quadrant facing outward, so the energy can flow outwards towards you and your environment.
- Intuitively select the next crystals and place them in whichever manner you are called to from each of the four quadrants and so on.
- Lastly, add the dried herbs in for an extra boost of Mother Earth herbal magic. Again, place these wherever you feel called to do so.
- Activate your grid by speaking your intention to it when you have completed its formation.

DARK MOON: END OF A CYCLE

Integrating knowledge, observance and rest

The dark moon is when there is zero illumination on the moon. This part of the moon cycle is less talked about than the others, but it is one of the most important in my opinion. The dark moon is the end of the lunar cycle where we integrate all of the knowledge we gained, observe the tests and trials we went through, and finally rest to experience true growth. If we don't take this important time to hit pause and rest, then we cannot fully integrate the experiences and wisdom we have gained. This integration is key to your recovery mentally, physically and emotionally.

Crystals for grounding

Grounding is an essential practice when you need to rebalance your mind, body and spirit. You can begin to heal and address important matters from a space of true clarity, focus and insight that you have gathered from grounding into Mother Earth. She will impart the wisdom for you to bring forward and accelerate your healing process and be still.

Dalmatian jasper – Known as the stone of service, Dalmatian jasper is used to maintain a balanced connection with your mind, body and spirit. Dalmatian jasper is wonderful for cleansing auras, dispelling any negative energies, grounding and deepening your connection to Mother Earth, and for protection, since it contains black tourmaline inclusions. Dalmatian jasper also encourages you to foster loyalty and faith into each and every relationship, by deepening your devotion to others.

Larvikite – Help to protect, ground and banish negative energies and strengthen your connection with Mother Earth, larvikite also enhances your psychic ability and helps you see yourself through the eyes of your higher self. Larvikite is said to increase brain function and allows you to easily absorb information in different ways than you have in the past. Larvikite's grounding presence helps you make those hard decisions in a rational manner not based upon emotion and clears your mind from harmful and chaotic thoughts.

Hematoid quartz – This crystal is a beautiful combination of hematite and quartz and it takes on the properties of each of those stones. Hematoid quartz is a powerful grounding crystal that allows your energies to stabilise and balances your thoughts and emotions, as well as removing negative energies from your body. It also has the ability to transmute these energies into healing white light. Use hematoid quartz when working on your root chakra, as it aids you in addressing matters to do with your shadow, while remaining grounded through the entire process.

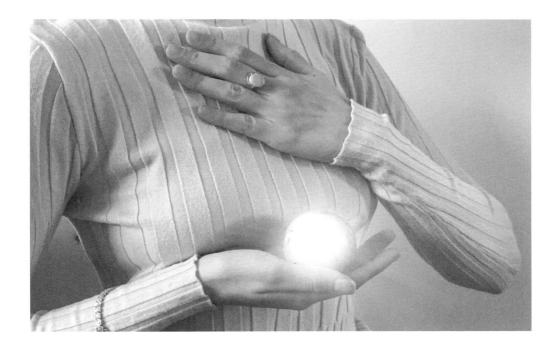

Dark moon ritual with grounding crystals

Create yourself a cosy, sacred space where you will be undisturbed. Grab your chosen grounding crystals and place them in your left hand, then place your right hand on your heart centre. Close your eyes and begin to pull your attention inwards by taking a full body scan for the areas that feel tense, as if you're holding on to something that is not yours or you no longer need to carry with you. These can be pent-up and unreleased emotions or trauma that has been stored in your body.

Once you have locked onto the areas in your human system that need releasing, it is time to breathe in deeply and exhale out three times. State to the dark moon that you are calling upon these tensions, these old emotions and traumas, to come forward and that you are now ready to release them. Repeat this process as many times as you feel necessary until you feel lighter and more relaxed.

Full body crystal healing and release

When I began to reawaken, I began to realise how much shadow and trauma I had suppressed from being a young child all the way through to adulthood. I thought this trauma hadn't affected me, when it clearly had major impacts on every decision I was making and what I was attracting and inadvertently calling into my life. When I started deep-diving inward and healing with crystals, all of my experiences with trauma, wounding and shadow started to pour out of me.

I allowed the crystals to guide me through this process of releasing what I was holding onto. I accepted their energetic gifts, and I used their frequencies to shift the emotional hurt and physical pain into something I hadn't recognised before: *joy*.

Three gorgeous stones that accelerated my crystal healing are opal, turquoise and samadhi quartz.

Opal – Known as the stone of the gods, opal pushes its owner and wearer to take responsibility for their feelings, past wounding, fear and resentments. It teaches you to let go of the negativity surrounding the behaviours you created to cope. Opal soothes your emotional body and helps you stay in control and also acts a shield from absorbing other people's negative energies and emotions. Opal fosters loyalty and faithfulness in its wearer. In the metaphysical world, opal brings the full spectrum of light energy into your system to clear your emotional body and boosts your will to live. Opal also enhances your cosmic consciousness and enhances your intuition and insight, while providing protection when you are doing inner work and shamanic journeys. Opal will bring all your traits to the surface for you to examine and do the work.

Turquoise – This is said to be one of the masters of the healing stones and can improve your overall mental state and provide you with protection against negative energy and vibrations. Turquoise acts as a gateway between the heavens and the Earthly realm, with the power to keep us completely grounded but fluid enough to be deeply connected to Spirit. Turquoise can induce energetic feelings of wholeness, serenity, emotional balance and good luck. Turquoise is also a programmable crystal, which means you can teach it a frequency to vibrate at and to set specific healing intentions.

Samadhi (pink Himalayan) quartz – This is a rare form of quartz, formed and found in the Himalayan Mountains of India and Nepal. Samadhi (pink Himalayan) quartz is considered to be one of the most powerful healing crystals and has been used for centuries in shamanic healing practices. It allows you to establish a clear connection with your guides, with its extremely high, but gentle vibration stimulating the third-eye chakra, allowing their information to be imparted to us. In turn, we can use this information as a healing tool.

Dark moon crystals – crystal healing ritual

This crystal healing process was created by my spirit guides and mentors who have guided me into my spiritual awakening. This process might seem hard the first couple of times you try it yourself – however, it gets easier the more you practise it. Feel free to omit some steps if you deem them unnecessary for yourself, as this is a process I use in my healing sessions with my clients. If you're having trouble doing this on yourself, you can also ask a trusted friend/healer to assist you.

What you need:

- A variety of crystals (I prefer to use tumbled stones and palm stones as they are smaller in size and stay on the body more easily) – twenty to thirty pieces
- A space you feel comfortable and relaxed in

- Some relaxing meditation music
- Essential oils and diffuser or incense to enhance your environment and state of deep relaxation to induce deep healing
- Chakra essential oils
- A pendulum
- A crystal roller
- Smudge stick, ethically sourced palo santo or smoke-less smudge spray

How to:
- Set up your environment by putting on your music, setting up your essential oil diffuser or lighting your incense sticks, and smudging in your preferred method to remove energies from the room.
- Gather your crystals, sit down comfortably and place them in front of you. Close your eyes and take three deep breaths. When you have completed your deep breaths, open your eyes.
- Intuitively select the crystals you are drawn to use during your healing and gridding process and put them in an easily accessible spot where you can reach them.
- Begin by gridding either the bottom half of your physical and etheric body or the top half of your physical and etheric body – start with where you have been called to.
- Using your chakra guide, begin placing crystals on your chakra system on your etheric body. Note that these placements will physically be on your body and outside of your body.
- After you have completed this step, using your intuition, start picking crystals and placing them on the points of your body where you feel have pain or you feel you need release or an energetic shift.

- Use your pendulum to balance and align the energy of the crystals and your physical and etheric system. Hold the pendulum above each crystal and let the pendulum circle and swing as it may – this means it is doing the work and assisting you to rebalance and activate. Once the pendulum has come to a halt, it is then time to move onto the next crystal. If you find that the pendulum doesn't move at all, don't be alarmed as this means it is already balanced and activated.
- Complete this process until you have done all the crystals on the first half of your body.
- Gently remove the crystals and thank them for rebalancing this portion of your body.
- Repeat these steps on the second half of your body.
- After the process has been completed on your entire body, it's time to gather your chakra essential oils. I use an essential oil set that targets each chakra – however if you don't have this available to you, use whichever essential oil you marry best with. *(Note – do not ingest these oils and read your labels to ensure they are able to be applied topically, as some essential oils can cause burning or irritation on the skin.)*
- Begin by placing a small drop of essential oil on the chakra point – starting from the root chakra.
- Grab your crystal roller and roll the essential oil into this area.
- Repeat this process until you have completed all the way up to the crown chakra.
- Once you have finished, cleanse your crystals from the energies they have absorbed during the healing process and give gratitude for them assisting you in healing.

Conclusion

I hope this book can bring you supportive guidance along your healing journey, as collating and passing down this information from the divine has done for me. My mission in this life is to help reawaken the collective and this is one more step in that journey.

As you participate in these rituals, address your shadow and build your confidence with these natural gifts from our Mother Earth, you are raising your vibrational frequency. In raising your own vibrational frequency, you single-handedly raise the frequency of the collective which brings us all closer as a stronger, more solid unit.

Remember that your journey is uniquely your own. Each and every step you take is a gift, and it is beautiful. From my guides to your human system, I wish you healing, joy and abundance for every aspect of your life here on this dimensional plane.

Disclaimer

Any information in this book is not intended or implied to be a substitute for professional medical advice, diagnosis or treatment. Always seek the advice of your doctor. This information is not intended to diagnose, treat, or cure any disease.

About the author

Leah is the owner of Dark Moon Crystals – an energy healing practice and crystal boutique. Leah intuitively hand-selects each crystal to ensure it contains the energetics aligned with the collective, and she can intuitively match you with your new crystal's specific vibrational frequencies.

Leah is also an intuitive crystal healer, light language healer and a channel. Everything she creates is a direct download from Source as she receives channelled messages and information that the collective needs to hear at the given time. Leah works with light-coded information that helps unlock sacred knowledge within your DNA to help instigate your awakening.

WWW.SHOPDARKMOONCRYSTALS.COM

@DARKMOON_CRYSTALS